TWAYNE'S WORLD AUTHORS SERIES

A Survey of the World's Literature

RUSSIA

Charles Moser, George Washington University

EDITOR

Nikolay Gumilev

TWAS 500

Nikolay Gumilev

NIKOLAY GUMILEV

By EARL D. SAMPSON
University of Colorado

TWAYNE PUBLISHERS
A DIVISION OF G. K. HALL & CO., BOSTON

891.7142
G974 S
1979

Library of Congress Cataloging in Publication Data

Sampson, Earl D.
Nikolay Gumilev.

(Twayne's world authors series ; TWAS 500 : Russia)
Bibliography: pp. 185–88
Includes index.
1. Gumilev, Nikolai Stepanovich, 1886–1921.
2. Poets, Russian—20th century—Biography.
PG3476.G85Z88   891.7'1'42   [B]   78–18006
ISBN 0–8057–6341–4

To Eleni

Contents

About the Author

Earl Sampson received his B.A. from the University of Colorado and his M.A. and Ph.D. from Harvard University. He is now an Associate Professor in the Department of Oriental and Slavic Languages and Literatures at the University of Colorado, where he has taught since 1963. His special interests are Russian poetry of the Silver Age, Pushkin, Russian versification, and the fiction of Vladimir Nabokov. His publications include articles on Gumilev, Nikolay Leskov, and Maria Pawlikowska.

Preface

The recent and growing revival of interest in the Acmeist school of Russian poetry has tended to concentrate primarily on two of the three major representatives of the school, Osip Mandelstam and Anna Akhmatova. This is probably as it should be, since they are undoubtedly more significant figures than the third member of the Acmeist trinity, Gumilev: Mandelstam is certainly a greater and more profound poet than Gumilev, and Akhmatova looms larger in the history of Russian poetry, in part because of her longer life (she was the only one of the three to survive the period of Stalinist suppression of the "decadent" Acmeist school, living to be recognized, toward the end of her life, as the *grande dame* of Russian letters) and the force of her moral-artistic example.

Still, however one may want to "rank" Gumilev in comparison to his Acmeist confreres, he is by any measure a major poet; furthermore, he was a highly influential figure in his time, as the chief organizer of the Acmeist grouping and as an indefatigable teacher and sponsor of younger poets. On both counts, he deserves more attention than he has so far received (at the time of preparation of this volume for the press, not a single monograph on Gumilev has yet appeared in English, and only one in any language: Marie Maline's *Nicolas Gumilev, poète et critique acméiste*). The present brief study does not aspire to be any more than a modest beginning toward filling this gap. My intent is to bring together in a reasonably comprehensive fashion the heretofore scattered information on Gumilev's personal and creative biography, insofar as it is presently available in print, and to provide what I hope is an integral interpretation and evaluation of the main body of his work. If this book can help to arouse a greater interest in Gumilev on the part of the scholar and the general reader of Russian poetry, and serve as a starting point for more comprehensive studies, my aim will have been achieved.

Since biographical information on Gumilev has heretofore

been scattered among various bio-bibliographical references, memoir articles, and prefaces to collections and selections of his work, I have begun with a fairly lengthy biographical chapter. The remainder of the book is a compromise between a chronological and generic organization of the material. Gumilev was a versatile writer, and practiced several genres, but his reputation and significance rest mainly on his lyrical poetry, in the Russian sense of a short, nonnarrative poem. Thus the central chapters of the book are devoted to this part of his *oeuvre*, divided into three chronological periods. The next chapter treats briefly his writings in other poetic genres, namely narrative poetry and dramatic poetry. Besides poetry, Gumilev also left a small body of prose: a dozen pieces of short prose fiction, some autobiographical prose, and some literary criticism and theory. However, I have chosen not to treat his prose in this book: the fiction and the autobiographical prose are of relatively little significance; the critical writings, on the other hand, are quite important, and deserve a fuller treatment than space would have allowed for here.

Gumilev's poetry has not been widely translated, and only recently has there appeared in English translation a selection of his work extensive enough to give the English-language reader a reasonably balanced idea of his *oeuvre*, namely the *Selected Works of Nikolai S. Gumilev* (Albany, 1972). Smaller selections of his poetry have appeared in English translation in *The Penguin Book of Russian Verse* and in Vladimir Markov and Merrill Sparks's *Modern Russian Poetry;* in 1945 a small volume entitled *The Abinger Garland,* consisting of translations of thirteen of his poems, was published as a special supplement to *The Abinger Chronicle* (Dorking, England). Since I have found it necessary to quote from quite a number of poems not represented in any of these sources, I have for the sake of consistency translated all quotations myself. However, so that the reader is not totally at the mercy of my renderings, I have indicated whenever a poem has also been translated in one of the volumes mentioned. In my own translations, my primary aim has been to provide, insofar as possible, a semantically accurate rendering of the Russian text; at the same time I have attempted to suggest, even if only faintly, something of the poetic texture of the original. Rhyme and meter are sacrificed to those two aims, although there are a few instances where the "correct" English words could be fitted into metrical and rhyming patterns without serious distortion of meaning. The line divisions of my translations correspond as closely as possible to the original, departing from this principle for the most part only when English and Russian syntax are at irreconcilable odds.

All quotations from Gumilev are from the four-volume *Sobranie sochinenii* (Collected Works), edited by G. P. Struve and B. A. Filippov and published by Victor Kamkin (Washington, D.C., 1962–68); citations are given in the body of the text, by Roman numeral for volume number and Arabic numeral for page numbers. In other references to this edition, the title will be abbreviated as SS.

In indicating rhyme schemes, I follow the Russian convention of using capital letters to indicate feminine rhyme and lower-case letters for masculine rhyme (e.g., AbAb).

I would like to thank Ardis Publishers for their kind permission to quote extensively from my article on *Pillar of Fire,* published in *Russian Literature Triquarterly,* no. 1 (Fall 1971), and to base the bibliography in this book on the bibliography published in the same issue. My thanks also go to Marilla Senterfit and Miss Jan Overton for their help in preparing the manuscript. And I owe a very great debt of gratitude to my wife, for her help and advice, for her patience, and for her constant encouragement.

Chronology

1886 Born April 3 (old style) in Kronstadt (Russia).

1902 First published poem.

1903– Completes secondary education in Tsarskoe Selo, where
1906 he meets the poets Innokenty Annensky and Anna Akhmatova. Publishes first book of verse, *The Path of Conquistadors* (1905).

1907– Studies in Paris at the Sorbonne. Publishes *Sirius*, a
1908 small literary magazine. Trip to Egypt and the Sudan (1907). Publishes second book of verse, *Romantic Flowers* (March 1908), and several short stories.

1909 Helps to found the artistic-literary journal *Apollon*. Trip to Abyssinia.

1910 Marries Akhmatova (April 25); honeymoon trip to Paris. Publishes third book of verse, *Pearls* (April). Trip to Abyssinia.

1911 Founds the Poets' Guild. Birth of son, Lev.

1912 Trip to Italy. Publishes fourth book of verse, *Foreign Skies* (April). Establishment of Acmeist school.

1913 Trip to Abyssinia and Somaliland. Publishes play *Actaeon* and writes narrative poem *Mik*.

1914 Publishes his translation of Gautier's *Émaux et camées*. Enlists in the army.

1915 Writes the play *The Child of Allah*. Twice awarded Cross of St. George for bravery in battle.

1916 Publishes fifth book of verse, *The Quiver* (January), and play *The Card Game*.

1917 Publishes play *Gondla*. Transferred to Paris. Writes play *The Poisoned Tunic*, and cycle of love poems published posthumously (1923); works on short novel *The Joyful Brotherhood*.

1918 Leaves army and returns to Russia. Divorced from Akhmatova. Publishes sixth book of verse, *The Pyre*, and book of adaptations from Chinese poets, *The Porcelain Pavilion*. Revives the Poets' Guild.

1919– Member of editorial staff of World Literature. Publishes
1921 translation of *Gilgamesh* and of other poetry. Teaches craft of poetry in various studios. Works on long poem *The Poem of the Beginning*. Marries Anna Engelhardt (1919). Birth of daughter, Elena (1920).

1921 Publishes seventh book of verse, *The Tent*. Arrested August 3; executed about three weeks later. Last book of verse, *The Pillar of Fire*, published shortly after his death.

CHAPTER 1

Gumilev's Life

I Childhood and School Years (1886–1906)

IN the early part of 1886, Stepan Yakovlevich Gumilev, a doctor in the Russian navy, was stationed on the island naval base of Kronstadt, in the Gulf of Finland. On April 15 of that year, his second wife, Anna Ivanovna, gave birth to their second son, Nikolay. The future poet's mother was the sister of an admiral, so that there was a naval tradition on both sides of his family; although Gumilev does not seem to have been attracted to a naval career himself, some of his poetry reflects his enjoyment of sea voyages, and a great admiration for the adventurous seafarers of earlier times. His sister-in-law believed that his boyhood imagination was fired by his father's stories of cruises to distant ports.[1]

If his birthplace was appropriate to the "Muse of Distant Travels" that Gumilev invoked more than once in his poetry, the town where he spent his early childhood was appropriate to the poetic muse: shortly after his birth, the family moved to Tsarskoe Selo, a city near St. Petersburg with strong poetic traditions. Russia's greatest poet, Alexander Pushkin, was educated at the imperial lyceum there, and remembered those years and that setting with affection in many of his poetic works (the town was renamed Pushkin in his honor in 1937). Two of Pushkin's classmates, Anton Delvig and Wilhelm Küchelbecker, also became poets, and many other poets resided in Tsarskoe Selo at some period of their lives, including Vasily Zhukovsky, Fedor Tyutchev, and Innokenty Annensky, and of course, Gumilev himself and his wife Anna Akhmatova.

From 1895 to 1900, the family lived in St. Petersburg, where the boys attended a private school.

According to one source, Gumilev began to write poetry and

stories at the age of eight.[2] A serious interest in poetry, however,
seems to have come somewhat later: his student and protégée,
Irina Odoevtseva, quotes him as having told her that poetry
"took possession" of him when he was fourteen, under the dual
impact of reading Pushkin's and Lermontov's poetry about the
Caucasus Mountains and seeing their wild scenery with his own
eyes.[3] The opportunity to see the Caucasus came in 1900 when
the poet's family moved to Tiflis (Tbilisi), where they stayed for
three years.

Although the incident is not confirmed in any other available
sources, B. P. Kozmin's biographical note relates that Gumilev
became interested in socialism while in Tiflis, read Marx, and
during a summer stay on his father's central Russian estate,
agitated among the flour-mill workers, thereby getting himself in
trouble with the provincial governor. Any Marxist leanings were
entirely a passing stage for Gumilev; a more significant and
better-documented biographical event of the Tiflis period is
the publication of a poem in a Tiflis newspaper in 1902, Gumilev's
first appearance in print, and his earliest extant verse.

In 1903 the family moved back to Tsarskoe Selo, and Gumilev
attended the secondary school there until his graduation in 1906.
The director of the school during almost all of Gumilev's stay
there was the poet Innokenty Annensky, a fact that may well
have been of considerable, though not necessarily crucial, importance in determining Gumilev's career. We don't really know
how close their association was during these years. However,
it is reported that Annensky read his pupil's work and encouraged
him to continue to cultivate his poetic gift,[4] and although it is
dangerous to use art as biography, Gumilev's later lines to the
memory of Annensky suggest that the impact of the older poet
on the student was a powerful one:

> He would let fall, as if by chance, a dozen
>   Strange and fascinating phrases,
> And they cast feeble me into a world
>   Of nameless dreams. (I, 211)

In any case, whatever the nature of the relationship may have
been, young Gumilev did not become Annensky's poetic disciple:

the book of verse that Gumilev published while still a student, at the age of nineteen, *Put' Konkvistadorov* (The Path of Conquistadors, 1905), shows not a trace of Annensky's influence.

In the meantime, Gumilev had made another acquaintance at Tsarskoe Selo, one of even greater significance in his biography: his schoolmate Anna Andreevna Gorenko, who later became his wife, and who is better known by her pen name—Akhmatova. Both poets later evoked their school-day romance in lines characteristic of each. Akhmatova veils the emotion, conveying it indirectly through the metonymic imagery of the setting:

> I was returning home from school,
> With books and a pencil-case in my book-strap.
> Those lindens have certainly not forgotten
> Our meeting, my cheerful boy. (1912)[5]

Gumilev speaks more directly of the emotion, and intensifies it with a literary and somewhat extravagant simile:

> Walking down the path, so strangely tender,
> A schoolboy and schoolgirl, like Daphnis and Chloe. (I, 163)

Of course, these lines tell us nothing very concrete, but they are worth quoting as the only direct witness we have from either participant on this first—and possibly happiest—phase of their tortured relationship. Even second-hand evidence on this point is sparse; we do have Sergey Makovsky's assertion that Gumilev spoke to him at times of the love he had felt toward Akhmatova since their adolescence.[6] Despite the reticence of both, it is clear that Gumilev's feeling for Akhmatova was deep and abiding, and her feeling for him possibly even more so, even though they found it impossible to establish a lasting and harmonious relationship. Its painful course is reflected a number of times in the poetry of both; one of the briefest and at the same time clearest and most touching revelations is found in the continuation of the lines just quoted from Akhmatova:

But the grey cygnet changed
When he became a haughty swan,
And across my life fell a ray
Of eternal sorrow, and my voice is muted.

II *Literary Apprenticeship (1906–1910)*

Many biographical sources speak of Gumilev as having been a poor student, and there is no reliable evidence to the contrary. His lack of academic success (he also studied at the Sorbonne and at the University of St. Petersburg without ever taking a degree) no doubt may be attributed at least in part to a strong commitment to literature and consequent lack of interest in other areas of endeavor. But some of his contemporaries considered that in general his intellectual powers were relatively limited, and it must be admitted that his poetry, whatever its other virtues, does not suggest a strong analytical brain or any great scholarly erudition. At any rate, whatever the causes, he must have had some difficulty in schoolwork, since he did not finish his secondary schooling until the late age of twenty. In spite of this, he went right on to university studies, enrolling in 1906 or 1907 at the Sorbonne. His sister-in-law's memoirs[7] imply that the choice of the Sorbonne rather than a Russian university might have been a compromise between his father's desire for him to continue his education (his father earned his own degree in spite of severe obstacles) and his own desire to begin the foreign travels that were to continue throughout his life. We know little about his studies in Paris beyond the fact that he attended lectures in Old French, French literature, and painting. But there are indications, from the variety of his other activities, that he did not take them very seriously. For one thing, in 1907 he published a small Russian literary-artistic magazine entitled *Sirius*. Although the magazine lasted for only three issues, it has the distinction of being the vehicle for Akhmatova's first appearance in print. Gumilev himself contributed much of the remaining material, writing poems and stories under the pseudonyms Anatoly Grant and K-o.

Also in 1907, Gumilev made his first trip to Africa, spending two months in Egypt and the Sudan. The trip was undertaken against his father's wishes, on money saved out of his expense allowance; he concealed it from his parents by writing a series of letters home before he left, which his friends mailed for him at regular intervals from Paris. It appears that he attempted to reduce his travel expenses by stowing away on a ship at the port of Trouville, but was discovered and arrested (this according to his sister-in-law;[8] Kozmin also records the arrest—"en état de vagabondage"—but does not mention a stowaway attempt).

His African impressions were soon reflected in his poetry, though in highly stylized form. In 1908, still in Paris, he published his second book of poetry, *Romanticheskie tsvety* (Romantic Flowers), dedicated to Anna Andreevna Gorenko. The "setting" for most of the poems in this collection is the same realm of absolute fantasy as in the poems of his first book, but a few have a locale that, in spite of the stylization, is identified or indentifiable as African or Egyptian.

From Alexey Tolstoy's 1921 memoir on Gumilev,[9] we know of one other significant incident from his Paris years—a suicide attempt. Tolstoy reports that as they sat together in a Paris sidewalk café in the summer of 1908, Gumilev told him how he went into the Boulogne woods and swallowed a dose of potassium cyanide—fortunately for him and for Russian poetry, a nonlethal dose. As to the reasons for the attempt, Tolstoy quotes Gumilev as follows: "You ask why I wanted to die. I was living alone, in a hotel—the thought of death pressed itself upon me. I found the fear of death unpleasant. . . . Besides, there was a certain girl here. . . ." We must remember that Tolstoy was reproducing the conversation after a thirteen-year interval, and that he may have allowed invention to aid memory. But if his report of Gumilev's words is at all accurate, the motives mentioned are extremely characteristic of the man. First there is the loneliness: throughout his life, and even at the height of his recognition as a poet and as a "maître"—a teacher and leader of other poets—Gumilev seems to have been a very lonely person, incapable of lowering his psychological defenses far enough to allow for close human contact. Although some of those closest to him attest to a kind, amiable, cheerful, and even playful side to his character in intimate circles, the impression remains that this conviviality was fairly superficial, and that no one really knew him very well. Then there is the idea of meeting head-on the challenge of fear, of giving radical proof of his courage, a theme that will run throughout both his life and his poetry. Next, there is the motive of an unhappy love experience (it is probable that the hint he made to Tolstoy related to Akhmatova's refusal of the proposal of marriage that he made to her before his departure for France). Like heroism, love is one of the major themes of his poetry and his biography. He seems to have been constantly in love with one woman or another and in need of a woman's love, but unable to find satisfaction therein, at least for any lasting period. Gumilev was endowed with powerful emotions, but due to some unfortunate twist in his psychological makeup—perhaps an inordinate fear of being emotionally hurt—was unable to give those emotions full expression and outlet. Even his poetry was but a partial, and for the most part circuitously indirect and heavily camouflaged expression of his emotional life. Furthermore, his psychology was clearly Romantic, and hence idealistic. Thus his love life worked under the double handicap of inhibition of his own feelings, and the inevitable disillusionment when the real women in his life fell short of the impossible Romantic ideal that he was always pursuing. (I should warn the reader that my analysis here is speculative, based less on solid evidence than on a variety of psychological hints in the memoir literature on Gumilev and to some extent—cautiously—on his poetry. It owes most to Odoevtseva's reminiscences and to Sergey Makovsky's assessment of his character.

Finally, the underlying theme of suicide itself is one that will appear fairly often in Gumilev's poetry, most appositely to this suicide attempt in the 1917 poem "Ezbekiah": ". . . ten years have passed / Since then . . . I was tormented by a woman then . . . I prayed to God for death then / And was ready to hasten it myself" (II, 30). And apparently the Paris incident was not the only occurrence of the sucide theme in actual life: his friend Georgy Ivanov speaks of a suicide attempt at the age of eleven.[10] Furthermore, his frequent courting of danger might be considered a concealed form of suicide attempt, the expression of a death wish. His return to Russia after the Revolution and his anti-Bolshevik activities have been interpreted in just this light.

By 1908, when Gumilev returned from France, he could consider his literary career auspiciously begun. At the age of twenty-two, he was the author of two collections of verse, both of which had been accorded the honor of sympathetic reviews by Valery Bryusov, the organizational leader of Russian Symbolism. Bryusov's review of *The Path of Conquistadors* had been quite reserved and critical in tone, but had ended on a positive note. His review of *Romantic Flowers* was much more encouraging: he saw in the book a considerable improvement in technique, and grounds for confidence in Gumilev's continued growth as a poet.

Back in Russia, Gumilev lived with his parents in Tsarskoe Selo. At his father's insistence, he enrolled in the University of St. Petersburg, but as before failed to take his studies seriously. Instead, he began to take a very active part in the literary-artistic life of Petersburg. Annensky, though no longer director of the school, was still living in Tsarskoe Selo, and Gumilev became quite close to him in the year or so of life remaining to him.

In January 1909, Gumilev made another acquaintance of great significance in his literary career, that of the art historian and critic Sergey Makovsky. Makovsky, at that time coeditor of the art review *Starye gody* (Ancient Years), was already planning a new literary-artistic monthly to fill the gap left by the disappearance, six years earlier, of Sergey Diaghilev's *Mir iskusstva* (The World of Art, an extremely influential "avant-garde" journal published from 1899 to 1903). Gumilev was very interested in the project, and made two signal contributions to its success: First, by interesting his older friend Annensky in the enterprise and introducing him to Makovsky, who, though a poet himself, was primarily an art specialist, and felt the need of a qualified and nonpartisan literary advisor for the planned journal. Annensky fulfilled that role brilliantly, and although he died with tragic suddenness in November 1909, after only one issue had appeared, Makovsky credits him with crucial contributions in the planning and organizing stages and in the preparation of the first two issues,[11] including a very significant three-part article on contemporary poets. Secondly, Gumilev himself was one of the most active and effective members of the editorial staff of the magazine, which was given the name of *Apollon* (Apollo). His major contribution to its pages, besides his own poetry, was a regular monthly article entitled "Letters on Russian Poetry," a review of current publications in Russian verse.

Besides his role in the foundation of *Apollon,* Gumilev was also active in another significant literary enterprise of the time, the formation of the group called the Academy of Verse and later renamed the Society of Adepts of the Artistic Word (Obshchestvo revnitelei khudozhestvennogo slova), a sort of permanent seminar on problems of poetry which existed for several years, brought together poets representative of widely differing tendencies, and provided the forum for the presentation and discussion of such significant papers as Vyacheslav Ivanov's "The Precepts of Symbolism" and Blok's "On the Present State of Russian Symbolism." Parallel functions were also carried out by *Apollon,* with which the society was closely associated.

A less successful enterprise undertaken by Gumilev in this period was the founding, together with A. N. Tolstoy, of a poetry magazine, *Ostrov* (The Island). The first issue appeared in April 1909, in a press run of only thirty copies. A second issue was prepared, but it is not clear whether it was actually published. There was no third issue. With the failure of the magazine, according to Tolstoy (see SS II, 361), Gumilev persuaded the director of a theater to entrust to him the editorship of the theater's playbill, which was thereupon transformed into a weekly poetry magazine. This stratagem worked for three issues before Gumilev was relieved of his editorial duties.

Meanwhile, along with all this literary activity, Gumilev found time to establish and uphold a reputation as a Don Juan. We know very few details of his love life in 1908–1909, but the memory of one brief affair has been preserved because it had as its consequence a well-established incident in Gumilev's life—his duel with the Symbolist poet Maksimilian Voloshin. In the winter of 1909, when a group of *Apollon* collaborators were gathered together, Voloshin quite suddenly and without obvious cause dealt Gumilev a powerful slap in the face. Gumilev tried to return the blow, and when the others present separated them, he challenged Voloshin to a duel. The seconds managed to work out the mild conditions of one shot each at twenty-five paces. Gumilev fired first and missed, and Voloshin's pistol misfired. Gumilev tried to insist that Voloshin take another shot, but the seconds refused. Thus the duel passed without injury, except to the participants' reputations, for the antimodernist press gave the "duel of decadents" a good deal of mocking publicity. The cause of Voloshin's attack was known for many years only to a few, but in 1955 Makovsky revealed it in print: the previous summer, Gumilev had had an affair with the minor poetess Elizaveta Dmitrieva, and had then cruelly insulted her; her close friend, Voloshin chose to avenge her honor by provoking Gumilev to a duel.[12] This is the only documented duel in Gumilev's life, although his sister-in-law makes reference to "two or three duels" that he told her of.[13]

The year 1910 was an eventful one in Gumilev's life. In the winter of 1909–10, according to Kozmin, he made a four-month trip to Abyssinia, to the city of Harrar. His father died early in the spring of 1910 after a long illness. On April 25, he and Akhmatova were married; the honeymoon was spent in Paris, and the rest of the summer on his mother's small estate of Slepnevo in the Tver province. Among the neighbors of the estate were several young people, including Vladimir and Vera Nevedomsky; Mrs. Nevedomsky has described, in her reminiscences of that and subsequent summers,[14] the young peoples' games and diversions, of which Gumilev was the chief inventor and instigator. For example, he organized a "circus," featuring himself as both ringmaster and daredevil trick-rider—though he was no expert horseman—and his wife as the "snake-lady," twisting her supple body into incredible positions (those who have seen photographs or portraits of the young Akhmatova will have no trouble believing this). He also invented for them the game of Characters, in which each participant chose a certain character type, such as the intriguer, the inquisitive, the brutally frank, etc., to sustain for several days, in all the situations of everyday life. This sometimes led to tense situations, particularly since the "actor's" real character was often opposed to the type he chose to portray. These two diversions, insignificant enough in themselves, are described for the light they throw on one of the traits in Gumilev's complex character: the compulsion to place himself in situations involving risk, whether physical or psychological.

In the fall, after the couple returned to Tsarskoe Selo, where they lived with his mother, Gumilev left behind his wife of less than a year and set out on a six-month trip through Abyssinia, where he hunted elephants and lions and collected Abyssinian folksongs and artifacts.

There is considerable confusion and conflicting testimony in regard to the number and dates of Gumilev's trips to Africa. Although many memoirists speak of three trips to Africa, the weight of evidence strongly indicates that there were four: the 1907 trip to Egypt and the Sudan, plus three separate trips to Abyssinia (1909–10, 1910–11, and 1913). First of all, there is a document in Gumilev's own hand, an official memorandum written in 1917, which says: "I have been in Abyssinia three times and all together spent almost two years in that country" (IV, 440). Similarly, in a note in *Apollon* during 1914 it is mentioned in connection with Gumilev's poem *Mik* that "The action of the poem takes place in Abyssinia, which Gumilev visited three times" (quoted in SS II, 336). Kozmin's note also mentions four different trips; unfortunately, through an apparent typographical error, two different trips are given the same date (1909–10), which may be one cause of the confusion.

Gumilev's third book of poetry, *Zhemchuga* (Pearls), was published in spring 1910, with the dedication "to my teacher, Valery Bryusov." This book brought him wide recognition and marked an even greater step forward in his poetic development than *Romantic Flowers*. With the publication of *Pearls*, Gumilev was no longer a beginner, but an established young poet of great promise, nearly ready to leave the phase of dependence on older masters and enter the phase of independence and originality; he was soon to break with his Symbolist teachers in order to found his own school, opposed to Symbolism: Acmeism.

III   *The Realization of a Goal and the Failure of a Dream (1911–1913)*

When he returned from Abyssinia in early 1911, Gumilev decorated the apartment in the house that he and Akhmatova shared with his mother, half-sister, brother, and sister-in-law with his exotic African souvenirs. The Gumilevs had an active social life in 1911, with many guests and literary soirees at home in Tsarskoe Selo, and many evenings spent in the Bohemian cafés of St. Petersburg, above all in the famous artistic cabaret with the name of the Stray Dog (*Brodiachaia sobaka*). The summer was spent again at Slepnevo. The summer company there and at neighboring estates included a number of attractive young women. Gumilev, unconstrained by his wife's presence, courted them all, but was particularly attracted to one, Mariya (Masha) Kuzmina-Karavaeva, a second cousin on his mother's side. This was apparently one of the stronger passions in Gumilev's life, though his sister-in-law surely exaggerates when she calls it "his most exalted and profound love."[15] The frail Masha died of tuberculosis the following year at the age of twenty-two, and although Gumilev did dedicate to her memory the poem "Rhodes" (*not* a love poem), written in that year, those who would make her the heroine of the 1921 poem "Zabludivshiisia tramvai" (The Streetcar Gone Astray) are almost certainly in error. We can probably accept Makovsky's statement, made on the authority of a relative of Masha's, that the poem "Devushke" (To a Young Girl) is addressed to her. In this piece, the poet calls her "a heroine of Turgenev's novels," and complains of her decorousness and her inability to understand his own impetuous and adventurous nature.

That winter, Akhmatova bore Gumilev a son, Lev, their only child.[16] Gumilev is reported to have spent the night of the delivery making the rounds of St. Petersburg taverns, in order to demonstrate his contempt for and superiority to the conventional conduct of expectant fathers.[17] On the other hand, he is said by his sister-in-law and others to have been a tender and solicitous father.

Meanwhile, Akhmatova was becoming known, not just as the wife of a poet, but as a poet in her own right. During 1911 she published poetry in *Apollon* and other periodicals; in the following year she published her first book of verse, *Vecher* (Evening). Gumilev at first opposed his wife's literary career, claiming to believe that poetry was not the business of women: see the lines in Akhmatova's poem "We met then for the last time": "He talked about the summer, and said/ That it's absurd for a woman to be a poet." Soon, however, he recognized her talent, relaxed his opposition, and often praised her work, both orally and in print; for example, in his review of *Chetki* (The Rosary), her second book.

By October 1911, then, when Gumilev organized a number of like-minded poets into the group he called the Poets' Guild (*Tsekh Poetov*; the word is used in its medieval meaning of a union of craftsmen), his wife, though still a beginner, could lay claim to professional membership in the group.

Gumilev shared the leadership of the Guild with a slightly older poet, Sergey Gorodetsky, but the major initiative for its establishment, and the major responsibility for the form and direction it took, were clearly his. Members, besides Gumilev, Gorodetsky, and Akhmatova, included Osip Mandelstam, Georgy Ivanov, Georgy Adamovich, Vladimir Narbut, Mikhail Zenkevich, Vasily Komarovsky, and others. The main thrust of the Guild was indicated by its name: Gumilev's intent was to bring together poets who, like himself, were strongly interested in poetry as craft.

The Guild was conceived and begun as a nonpartisan group, but the major issue of the regular meetings held during the winter of 1911–12 was the formation of another and definitely partisan group, which put itself forward under the name of Acmeism as a new school of poetry. The Acmeist school continued the Guild's concern with the problems of the craft of poetry, but its major historical significance lay in its opposition to Symbolism, the school that had dominated Russian poetry since the turn of the century, but was now on the decline as an organized movement and as a progressive, creative force. In the view of the Acmeists, Symbolism had carried to an extreme the mystical, otherworldly tendencies implied in its label, and had laid excessive emphasis on the musical values of poetry, the allusive and elusive techniques of melody, atmosphere, suggestion, and nuance. To these, Acmeism opposed a concern for the concrete world of everyday reality, for pictorial and plastic values, and for the precise and logical use of the poetic word. Thus it combined what might be called neo-Classical and neo-Realistic tendencies, in opposition to the neo-Romanticism that dominated in the Symbolist movement.

The Acmeists found a sympathetic forum in *Apollon*, which published the first official manifestos of the group in its January 1913 issue, but *Apollon* was not, in 1912, nor did it ever become, an exclusively Acmeistic journal. Thus, to provide themselves with their own group organ, the Acmeists established in 1912, under the organizational aegis of the Poets' Guild, the publishing firm of Hyperboreus, and a journal by the same name, which appeared during 1912 and 1913.

The major event in Gumilev's literary career in 1912, together with the realization of his goal of founding a new school of poetry, was the appearance of his fourth book of verse, *Chuzhoe nebo* (Foreign Skies). This is the collection that most fully exemplifies Gumilev's Acmeistic theories, but more importantly, it is his first truly original book, the first that does not suggest imitation of any older poets. It is not the "acme" of his career, since his poetry was to undergo a considerable evolution in the nine years remaining to him, but it is from this point forward that he clearly stands on his own two feet as a poet.

In the spring of 1912, Gumilev and Akhmatova made a tour of Italy, a trip which inspired a series of fine poems on Italian themes by Gumilev, and a few by Akhmatova. The summer was again spent at Slepnevo. The winter was occupied, aside from serious literary work, by the same *vie-de-Bohême* and literary soirees, both at home and in the St. Petersburg cabarets, as the previous winter.

According to Kozmin's note, Gumilev enrolled in the department of Romance and Germanic Philology of the University of St. Petersburg in the fall of 1912, in order to study Old French poetry, although his sister-in-law tells us that he had enrolled immediately upon his return from Paris in 1908.[18] The most likely explanation is that he had dropped his studies after a year or so and now, in 1912, decided to renew them.

The year 1913 began with the "official" launching of Acmeism— although it had already been in existence for several months—via the publication in *Apollon* of Gumilev's manifesto "Acmeism and the Legacy of Symbolism" and Gorodetsky's "Some Currents in Contemporary Russian Poetry."

In his poem "Abyssinia," published in 1921 but possibly written earlier, Gumilev wrote: "There is a Museum of Ethnography in this city . . . I go there to touch the savages' objects / That I once brought myself from afar" (II, 89). The background to these lines is Gumilev's last trip to Africa, which occupied the spring and summer of 1913. His previous trips had been made at his own expense, but this time he went as one of the leaders of an ethnographical expedition to Abyssinia, Gallaland, and Somaliland, sponsored by the Russian Academy of Sciences. One of the purposes of the expedition was the compilation of collections of artifacts of the area, and the items that the expedition brought back were put on display in the academy's Museum of Anthropology and Ethnography in Petersburg. To this day, on the wall of the African room of that museum, there hangs a map showing the itinerary of that expedition and bearing the name of N. Gumilev.

Gumilev also speaks of his African souvenirs in another poem, the important autobiographical piece entitled simply "Iambic Pentameters": "But the months passed, I sailed / Back, bringing elephant tusks, / Pictures by Abyssinian artists, / Panther skins— I liked their spots . . ." (I, 222). A little further on, the poet speaks of returning from Africa to find that he had lost her for whom he had "sought the imperishable purple of royal robes." Some sources, perhaps under the influence of this poem, date a final break between Gumilev and Akhmatova to his return in 1913. But this part of the poem was written *before* his last trip, and there exist other indications that the estrangement had reached the point of virtual or actual separation before their marriage was three years old. The external history of this estrangement remains quite vague. One of the factors that makes it difficult to pin down dates is that for some time after the break with Gumilev, Akhmatova apparently maintained close ties with his mother, probably on account of her son. According to Gumilev's sister-in-law, the boy's grandmother had the major responsibility for his care and upbringing from the beginning;[19] this was still true in the years between the divorce in 1918 and Gumilev's death. Thus, for example, Akhmatova spent the summers of 1913 through 1916 on her mother-in-law's estate.

If the facts of the estrangement are still unknown, the causes are not difficult to guess. These two poets, these two strong and proud temperaments—the one demonstratively proud, to the point of arrogance, the other more quietly but nonetheless deeply proud—were bound to clash. By all accounts, there was a good deal of self-centered egotism in Gumilev's nature, and he must have been a difficult man for any woman to live with. He wanted to preserve his male independence, his freedom to set off alone on long and dangerous expeditions, and, it must be said, his freedom to transgress at will the bounds of marital fidelity. Such, at least, is the picture given by any number of contemporaries; if it is an exaggeration, it is on the conscience of those memoirists. Akhmatova, on the other hand, was not the sort of woman to submit passively to such treatment; furthermore, as a poet, a remarkable and profound artist, she had far too rich a spiritual life of her own to find her fulfillment in feminine self-sacrifice to the whims and glory of her husband.

No doubt some day more light will be thrown on this relationship by the discovery or release of family archives. Whatever changes this light may occasion in the picture I have drawn, I feel sure that it will confirm that the separation, inevitable as it may have been, was a painful one on both sides. Makovsky, speaking of the approaching rift, says that he "felt she was already a part of himself, his incarnate dream."[20] One of the many poetic testaments to the pain of their parting that could be cited from the poetry of both are these simple lines from a poem first published in *Foreign Skies:* "You couldn't call her beautiful, / But in her lies all my happiness" (I, 165).

IV *War and Revolution (1914–1918)*

Along with his activities as a leader of the Poets' Guild and the Acmeists, Gumilev continued to participate in the Society of Adepts of the Artistic Word. At a December 1913 meeting of the society, he read his one-act play *Actaeon,* and at a February 1914 meeting, he read his long narrative poem *Mik.* At the same meeting, he presented his views on epic poetry, and there was general discussion on his poem and on his theoretical views.

Another important event in Gumilev's literary life in early 1914 was the appearance in print of his complete translation of Théophile Gautier's *chef d'oeuvre,* the collection of verse *Émaux et Camées.* Gautier was one of Gumilev's favorite poets: he had published an article on him in *Apollon* in 1911, accompanied by translations of four of his poems, which were also included in *Foreign Skies.* In his manifesto of Acmeism he had included Gautier in a list of the poets most highly admired in Acmeist circles.

From *The Path of Conquistadors* on, Gumilev had celebrated in his verse the principles of personal courage and strong will; he was fond of stating that the central tenet of his conduct, as well as his poetry, was to follow the path of maximum resistance. When war was declared on Russia on August 1, 1914, he saw in this an opportunity to put his principles into practice in a cause more significant than the collection of exotic regalia and hunting trophies, and to give practical expression to his deeply felt patriotism. He rejected the opportunity taken by other artists and intellectuals to contribute to the war effort by means of safe rear-echelon or civilian activities, and despite a medical certificate that would have exempted him from all military service, he alone of the prominent Russian men of letters volunteered for combat duty. He enlisted as a private in the Empress Alexandra's Guards Regiment of Uhlans, and reported to his unit in September. He saw action first in Prussia, against the Germans, and later in Poland, on the Austro-Hungarian front. He proved to be an excellent soldier, fought bravely, in spite of a rather weak constitution, and for his valor in battles of January 1915 was awarded two St. George Crosses—he said of himself in a poem of 1921, "But St. George twice touched / His breast, untouched by bullets" (II, 36)—and promoted to the rank of noncommissioned officer. In April 1916, he was promoted to 2nd lieutenant (*praporshchik*) and transferred to the Empress Alexandra's 5th Hussar regiment. He described some of his combat experiences and impressions in a series of front-line reports that appeared under the heading "Zapiski Kavalerista" (Notes of a Cavalryman) in *Birzhevye vedomosti* (Stock-Exchange News) from February 1915 to January 1916.

After the initial campaigns of fall and winter 1914–15, Gumilev apparently was able to leave the front for Petrograd fairly often. Makovsky claims to have met with him several times in the summers of 1915 and 1916;[21] he read some of his poetry at a December 1915 meeting of the Society of Adepts of the Artistic Word; and in March 1916 he gave a reading of his new verse play *Ditia Allakha* (The Child of Allah).

Gumilev also found time in 1916 to write another verse play, *Gondla.* The play was published the following year in Peter Struve's prestigious journal *Russkaya mysl* (Russian Thought), to which Gumilev had been a frequent contributor since 1912.

Nineteen sixteen was also the year of publication of Gumilev's fifth book of poetry, *Kolchan* (The Quiver). For most contemporaries, the main interest of this collection probably lay in the remarkable war poems that it included, in which Gumilev celebrates war as a trial of the spirit, "as a serious, stern and holy affair, in which the whole force of an individual soul and the total value of a determined human will are revealed before the face of death."[22] The considerable poetic power of these war poems is still evident, but for the present-day reader their decorative imagery and rhetoric may have a somewhat artificial ring, and now we would probably not want the book's reputation to rest on them, since along with them we find many poems on other themes, of equal or greater quality. For us, the major significance of the book must lie in the new direction in Gumilev's development that it shows, the greater depth and maturity of artistic thought. *The Quiver* made it clear that the significance of Gumilev's poetry was not to be confined to the exemplification of his rather narrow Acmeistic theories; in it we can clearly see him moving toward the more complex and less easily classified poetic system of his late work.

Between August and October 1916, Gumilev was attached to the cavalry school in Petrograd, for the purpose of taking an examination for promotion. He failed the exam and returned to his regiment in the same rank, which he held for the remander of his military service.

In the spring of 1917, after the March Revolution, Gumilev was transferred from the Eastern front, with orders to join the Russian brigades at Salonika. Given his restless nature, it is possible that he was disillusioned with the growing disorganization and inactivity of the Russian army and himself requested the transfer to a more active theater of the war. He left Russia in May, and traveled via Finland, Sweden, Norway, and England (he stayed over briefly in London and made some literary acquaintances there) to Paris, where he arrived in July. For some reason, perhaps connected with the lull on the Salonika front, his orders were changed, and instead of continuing to Salonika, he was attached to the Provisional Government's Military Commissariat in Paris. He stayed six months in Paris, went from there to London, where he spent nearly three months, and then returned to Russia.

Gumilev's stay in Paris was marked above all by his passion for Elena D., a young woman of half-Russian, half-French descent. He expressed this passion in a series of love poems that he wrote in her album. After his death in 1923, these poems were published under the title *K sinei zvezde* (To the Blue Star), after the title of one of them, in which he addresses his beloved as a blue star. His feelings for her were not reciprocated, and Elena married an American, a fact that Gumilev recorded ironically in a three-line poem entitled "Tanka:"

> And now the girl with the eyes of a gazelle
> Is marrying an American—
> Why did Columbus discover America? (II, 166)

This "tanka"—a very brief Japanese verse form—is the least serious fruit of the active interest in Oriental poetry that Gumilev pursued at this time. He collected anthologies and studies of Oriental poetry, and put this material to creative use in a small collection of adaptations from various Chinese and Indo-Chinese poets that he published in 1918 under the title *Farforovyi pavil'on* (The Porcelain Pavilion).

Besides the Chinese and Indo-Chinese traditions—and the Japanese, if we include the tanka—several other "Eastern" poetic traditions left their traces in his work. The Malaysian is represented by two pantoums (a series of quatrains rhyming, ABAB, BCBC, CDCD, etc.) one incorporated into his play *The Child of Allah* and one, written in 1917, devoted to a characterization of the art of his friends Mikhail Larionov and Natalya Goncharova, with whom he met frequently during his stay in Paris. Although his interest in poetic Orientalia was strongest in 1917, it began earlier, as shown by the pantoum in *The Child of Allah* and by two ghazels, or Persian lyric poems, incorporated into the same play; and continued afterward, as shown by the poems "Imitation of the Persian" and "The Drunken Dervish" from his last collection of verse, *The Pillar of Fire*, and by his 1919 translation of the Babylonian epic *Gilgamesh*.

Much of the information we have on Gumilev's activities in Paris and London comes from some personal papers that he left with a friend in London on his return trip. These papers are now in the hands of the prominent Russian émigré scholar Professor Gleb Struve, who has published most of them, with careful commentary.

Among those papers is a short memorandum (IV, 439–40) characterizing the various tribes of Abyssinia from the point of view of their military potential, describing the political organization of the country, noting some of the advantages of recruitment of volunteers there, and outlining Gumilev's personal experience with Abyssinia. It is not clear whether the memorandum was prepared on request, as the Allied commands did in fact give some consideration to the recruitment of African legions, or on Gumilev's own initiative, nor do we know whether it was actually submitted, and if so, what consideration it received. In any case, Gumilev must have soon abandoned the hope—which we can read between the lines of the memorandum— of being sent on a mission to Abyssinia, for at the very beginning of 1918 he requested to be attached to the British army fighting in Mesopotamia. The request was approved by the Russian authorities in Paris, and toward the end of January he left for London. But again, as with the Salonika assignment, he failed to reach his destination, for unknown reasons. It would appear that his intent from the time he left Paris was to return to Russia if the Mesopotamian assignment did not work out, for two days after his arrival in London he received an advance of travel money for the trip from London to Petrograd.[23] He remained in London nearly three months, however, presumably trying to gain approval from the British authorities to join their forces in Persia. But in April he sailed for Russia, and arrived in Petrograd in May. He had been gone exactly a year, leaving shortly after the "bourgeois" revolution of March 1917, and returning nearly six months after the November revolution that installed the Bolsheviks in power. We have no record of his reactions to the events of 1917, but his attitude toward the new regime was soon to come clear.

V *"In the Middle of the Journey of Life"* (1918–1921)

Throughout his life, Gumilev displayed an amazing capacity for refusal to allow external circumstances to affect his spiritual state or interfere with his work. We have seen the level of literary activity that he managed to maintain during the war years; it is still more surprising to see what he did during the three years and three months that he lived in Soviet Russia. Always energetic, always optimistic and resolute, he maintained these qualities throughout the difficult years of War Communism. A number of people who lived through this period in St. Petersburg have attested to the unusually charged spiritual atmosphere of the times. It is as though, deprived by the dislocations of revolution and civil war of all but the most elementary conditions of material well-being, the artists and intellectuals turned all the more avidly to spiritual sustenance. But Gumilev displayed an energy and work-capacity that was unusual even for those times; reading the reports of his multifarious activities, one wonders how he managed to fit it all into a twenty-four-hour day. Besides writing and publishing a good deal of his own poetry, he worked as a translator and editor, taught courses and read lectures in a wide variety of educational institutions, was active in several literary organizations, gave poetry readings, and, finally, during the last months of his life, was apparently involved in counterrevolutionary activities.

Very shortly after his return from abroad, an important change took place in Gumilev's personal situation when his six-year estrangement from Akhmatova culminated in a divorce. That year or the next he married Anna Nikolaevna Engelhardt, who had been in love with him since before his trip to Paris. The following year, in 1920,[24] she bore him a daughter, Elena, a name Gumilev chose possibly in honor of his unrequited Parisian love. Both mother and daughter perished in the siege of Leningrad during the Second World War.

In 1918, *Apollon* was already defunct and Gumilev, now a civilian, had no regular income other than his royalties. According to Ivanov, he had previously lived on income from family property,[25] but of course this income was now cut off. Perhaps this explains, at least in part, why 1918 was his most active year in terms of publication. The most important publication of that year was a new book of poetry (his sixth), *Koster* (The Pyre). Also in 1918, he published his long poem *Mik*, written several years earlier but not previously published; *The Porcelain Pa-*

vilion; a separate edition of his play *The Child of Allah,* which had previously appeared in *Apollon;* and finally, second, revised editions of *Romantic Flowers* and *Pearls.* New editions of *Foreign Skies* and *The Quiver* were announced but did not appear.

Of the variety of Gumilev's activities in 1918–21, the one that occupied the greatest amount of his time and energy—and presumably provided the major portion of his income—was probably his work with Maxim Gorky's translating and publishing enterprise, World Literature (Vsemirnaia literatura). Gorky's intent in establishing World Literature at the end of 1918 was twofold: to provide a large number of writers and scholars, dislocated by the Revolution, with regular employment; and to contribute to raising the cultural level of the Russian masses by means of comprehensive series of translations of the classics of world literature. The rather grandiose initial plans of the enterprise were not fulfilled, but while it lasted, World Literature admirably fulfilled Gorky's aims for it.

Upon the formation of World Literature, Gumilev was chosen a member of its governing board, in charge of the French literature section, and also coeditor, with his friend Mikhail Lozinsky, and with Alexander Blok, of the poetry series. Besides his editorial duties, Gumilev did a good deal of translation himself. In 1919, World Literature published his translation of Coleridge's *The Rime of the Ancient Mariner,* with a foreword by Gumilev; and a book entitled *The Principles of Artistic Translation,* which contained articles on translation by Gumilev ("On Verse Translations"), Korney Chukovsky, and F. D. Batyushkov. Also in 1919, the Grzhebin publishing firm published his translation of *Gilgamesh,* with a translator's foreword by Gumilev and an introduction by his collaborator in the translation, the Assyriologist Vladimir Shileyko, who was, incidentally, Akhmatova's second husband. Other World Literature editions that Gumilev edited and/or contributed translations to include the ballads of Robert Southey, a collection of traditional Robin Hood ballads, and editions of Heine, Voltaire, and Oscar Wilde. He also translated and edited a small anthology of French folksongs which was issued by the Petropolis publishing firm in 1923. Earlier, before the war, Gumilev had translated from Villon, Vielé-Griffin, and Robert Browning, as well as Gautier.

The period of the New Economic Policy (NEP) was characterized by the coexistence of state enterprise and private enterprise. This extended into the publishing business: alongside such state-sponsored firms as World Literature, there were a number of private publishers, most very ephemeral, but some quite significant. Among the most significant were the two mentioned in the preceding paragraph, the firm of Z. I. Grzhebin and the Petropolis firm. The former, another of Gorky's projects, was founded in 1919, thus anticipating somewhat the NEP period. Gumilev was an editorial consultant for Grzhebin. It is not clear how extensive his duties there were, but he did edit a volume of selected works of Alexey Konstantinovich Tolstoy. The book was published in 1923, with a foreword by Gumilev. It was designated Volume I, but no further volumes of the projected series ever appeared. Grzhebin also published the second edition of Gumilev's *The Pyre* (1922), and his translation of *Gilgamesh*.

The World Literature undertaking was a very characteristic phenomenon of Russian, and especially of Petersburg's cultural life in those first years after the Revolution; no less characteristic was the proliferation of educational enterprises, literary and artistic studios, lecture series, etc. In the words of Irina Odoevtseva, "there was a vast number of courses at that time—everything from book-binding and chicken-raising to the study of Egyptian and Sanscrit inscriptions. It was possible to study—free of charge—anything you might want."[26] These courses and studios provided Gumilev with another field of activity, one particularly well suited to his constant drive to teach, to lead, to pass on his knowledge and infect others with his enthusiasm for poetry.

The first such organization that Gumilev became involved with was the Institute of the Living Word (Institut zhivogo slova). Founded at the end of 1918 by the prominent actor and historian of Russian theater Vsevelod Vsevelodsky-Gerngross, the Living Word, as it was informally called, was primarily a theater studio, but it included a "literary section," in which Gumilev was invited to teach the theory and practice of poetry. His first lecture took place in November 1918, and he continued to teach there until the end of 1920. The Institute itself continued in existence until 1923.

Another important rostrum for Gumilev's teaching activities was the Literary Studio, sponsored by the House of Arts. In summer 1919, at Gumilev's suggestion, a studio was established in conjunction with World Literature. The main intent was to train young writers for translation, but when it proved that the students were more interested in original writing, which was beyond the purview of World Literature, sponsorship of the studio was transferred to the House of Arts in December 1919. The courses in the Literary Studio were divided into two types, lecture course and workshop; Gumilev taught a lecture course in dramaturgy and led the workshop in poetic technique. Among his students in the studio were Irina Odoevtseva, who emigrated with her husband, Gregory Ivanov, in 1922 and became one of the leading émigré poetesses; Vladimir Pozner, born in France but educated in Russia, who re-emigrated and became a French author; Lev Lunts, an extremely talented and promising writer who died young, in 1924; and Nikolay Chukovsky, who died in 1965 after a distinguished career in Soviet letters.

Besides his regular courses at the Living Word and the Literary Studio, Gumilev read lectures at a number of other institutions, including the Institute of the History of the Arts, Proletcult (Proletarian Culture), Baltflot (Baltic Fleet), and a Red army group. Several memoirists have commented on his refusal to compromise his political convictions, or even to make any attempt to keep them to himself before such audiences as the last three mentioned, and in the necessary dealings with their Communist organizers. For example, when he gave a reading of his African poems to a Baltflot group one evening, he chose to include the poem "Galla," with its lines "I gave him [a tribal leader] a Belgian pistol / And a portrait of my emperor" (II, 91). According to Odoevtseva, who was in attendance, these lines occasioned a rumble of discontent, but Gumilev pretended not to notice, and outfaced his audience, who rewarded his courage with an outburst of applause. Gumilev admitted afterwards to Odoevtseva that he was frightened, but he believed that courage consists in victory over fear, rather than lack of fear. "Only a fool," she quoted him, "doesn't see danger and isn't afraid of it."[27]

The House of Arts (Dom iskusstv) was another characteristic phenomenon of the time, one Gumilev was closely associated with. It was founded in 1919 by Gorky, with the support of the Commissariat of People's Education, at first with the purely practical aim of providing some artists and writers with living and dining accommodations, but it quickly expanded its scope to include such activities as the Literary Studio, art exhibitions, concerts, and literary soirees. During 1920, two of its evenings were devoted to Gumilev's readings of his own poetry. He was a member of its council from its founding until March 1921, and in spring 1921 he and his wife took up residence there. It was in his apartment there that he was arrested in August.

According to Professor Struve, another of Gorky's aims in establishing the House of Arts was to counterbalance the influence of the "bourgeois" House of Writers (Dom literatorov),[28] a similar organization founded in late 1918, whose membership consisted mainly of older and more established writers. But there were those who were associated with both Houses, and Gumilev was one of them. He was a member of the steering committee of the House of Writers in 1920 and 1921, and gave poetry readings there in the same years. His next-to-last address—No. 5 Preobrazhensky Street (now Radishchev Street)—was quite close to the House of Writers on Basseyny Street (now Nekrasov Street), and he visited the house frequently at that time, more so than after he moved into the House of Arts, located on the corner of Nevsky Prospect and the Moyka Canal.

In June 1920 the young poetess Nadezhda Pavlovich, a Communist-party member, arrived in Petersburg, charged with the task of organizing the Petersburg section of the All-Russian Union of Poets, a semiofficial grouping. Gumilev took part in the organizational meeting, at which Alexander Blok was chosen chairman. According to Odoevtseva,[29] it soon became clear to those of the members of the union who were not Bolshevik sympathizers that Blok was a figurehead chairman, and that the real power was in the hands of Pavlovich, who of course tried to guide the union along lines agreeable to the party. Gumilev led an opposition group, which demanded a new election of officers on parliamentary grounds. The new election took place that fall, and Gumilev was elected chairman in Blok's place; he remained chairman until his death.

Gumilev's motives in challenging Blok for the chairmanship of the union were probably manifold. Besides the idealistic purpose of turning, as Odoevtseva puts it, "the intense activity of the Union to the profit of the poets" (as opposed to the party), he was quite likely motivated also by the personal consideration of adding to his own influence and prestige. He seems to have been almost obsessively driven in these last years to extend his influence and fame in every possible direction. Finally, his poetic rivalry with Blok may also have played a role. Although the latter consideration was probably a minor one here, this is a convenient place to comment on that rivalry, which was at its most intense in the years just preceding the deaths of the two poets, which occurred so strangely close together. From 1918 to 1921, Blok was quite clearly the most popular and prestigious of Russia's poets, and Gumilev, with his unbounded ambition, could not but take this as a challenge to his own prestige. Many contemporaries have commented on the division in those years of the poetic world, at least in St. Petersburg and in St. Petersburg–oriented circles—Moscow was another matter—into two camps: the followers of Blok and the followers of Gumilev. The rivalry had its roots in Gumilev's championship of Acmeism as an opponent of Symbolism, and although by 1918 the struggle of the two "isms" as such was no longer an issue,[30] the basic principles that had underlain that struggle were still pertinent. Blok was still seen as the leading representative of the mystical, oracular, and Dionysian view of poetry; Gumilev as the standard-bearer of the more realistic, craft-oriented and Apollonian attitude. As so often happens in such cases, the practice of each poet was to some degree at odds with his own theory, and as a result the two adversaries were more sharply opposed in theory than in practice; still, the differences between them were clear and significant. The tradition, established in those years, of juxtaposing the names of Blok and Gumilev has proved to be quite tenacious, and although it has its valid critical bases, it is clear that the coincidence of the two poets' deaths has helped sustain it.

All those official and semiofficial positions provided Gumilev's material support and helped expand his influence and prestige. But from what we know of his personality—his ambition, his talents for organization, his zest for leadership, and the pleasure he derived from working with young poets—we can assume confidently that his heart lay first of all with the several poetic circles that he personally organized and led during these years. His favorite, most likely, was the reconstituted Poets' Guild, usually referred to as the Second Guild. Some sources state that it was founded as early as 1918, but Odoevtseva gives 1920.[31] Whereas the first Guild was made up mainly of poets who were Gumilev's approximate coevals and more or less his equals in terms of literary experience and public recognition, the ranks of the second Guild were made up mostly of considerably younger, just-beginning poets, such as Irina Odoevtseva, Nikolay Otsup, Vsevelod Rozhdestvensky, and others (although there were also those closer to Gumilev's age: Georgy Ivanov, Georgy Adamovich). Thus his role in the second Guild was more clearly that of leader and poetic mentor of young talents—a role that he seems to have enjoyed. Besides foregathering for literary discussion, the new Guild sponsored publications. Gumilev's collection of verse *The Tent* appeared under the imprint of the Poets' Guild, and one issue of the Guild's miscellany appeared before his death, under the title *The Dragon* (1921). Three more numbers appeared after his death. Besides the miscellany, in 1921 the Guild put out four issues of a journal, *The New Hyperboreus,* in miniscule hectographed editions.

A similar but apparently somewhat broader, less exclusively "Acmeistic," group that Gumilev founded was the circle called the Sounding Sea-Shell (*Zvuchashchaia rakovina*). Members included Nikolay Tikhonov and Vera Lourie. Nina Berberova, later a prominent émigré writer, joined the group at its last meeting preceding Gumilev's arrest. At its founding, the circle was also associated with World Literature, then became an independent group. The circle ostensibly closed after Gumilev's execution, but continued to exist unofficially for another year, and published an album of the members' poetry, dedicated to Gumilev, in autumn 1921.

Gumilev's last such initiative was the formation in July

1921 of the House of Poets, apparently on the model of the House of Arts and the House of Writers. Its quarters were in Liteyny Prospect, at the same address as the Union of Poets, so there was probably some connection between them.

In June 1921, Gumilev participated in a train trip to Sevastopol and a cruise on the Black Sea. He returned to Petersburg in July, tanned, healthy, and in top spirits; the optimism and buoyancy that impressed so many contemporaries during his last years were at a peak. He felt himself in the prime of his physical and creative life, his prestige was great and growing, his multitude of activities were, in the main, prospering and bringing him great satisfaction, and he was proud of and pleased with his two growing children. While in Sevastopol he had arranged the publication of his "poetic geography" *Shater* (The Tent), a cycle of African poems, and he was now preparing for the press another collection, the projected title of which reflected his state of mind: "In the Middle of the Journey of Life" ("Posredine stranstviia zemnogo," a translation of the opening line of *The Divine Comedy*). He was fond in these weeks of stating his expectation of living to an age of ninety or so.

All this was brought to an abrupt end in the early morning of Wednesday, August 3, when he returned to his apartment in the House of Arts from a meeting of the Sounding Sea-Shell, to find agents of the Cheka waiting for him with search and arrest warrants. He took two books to prison with him: the Bible and Homer. Four days later, August 7, Gumilev's great rival Blok died. At the cemetery after Blok's burial on August 10, a deputation was formed to request Gumilev's release on the surety of several organizations, including the Academy of Sciences, World Literature, Proletcult, and others; the delegation included Nikolay Otsup, A. L. Volynsky, N. M. Volkovyssky, and the secretary of the Academy of Sciences, S. F. Oldenburg. The request was turned down, and the delegation was unable to learn anything about the charges or expected proceedings. Although they received assurances of his immediate safety, during the last week of August rumors of his execution circulated in St. Petersburg—rumors which were confirmed on September 1,

when the newspaper *Petrograd Pravda* carried a notice about
the discovery of an antigovernment conspiracy and the execution before a firing squad of sixty-one conspirators, including
"Gumilev, Nikolay Stepanovich, 33 [this is of course an error;
he was 35—E.S.], former member of the gentry, philologist, poet,
member of the governing board of World Literature Publishing
House, nonparty, former officer."[32] The date of the Petrograd
Cheka's decree of execution was August 24, but the date on
which it was carried out, and thus the exact date of Gumilev's
death, remains—like his place of burial—unknown. It was probably August 24 or 25, the two dates most often cited in various
sources, but August 23, August 27, and even the 30th or the 31st
have also been cited. Gorky is said to have appealed directly
to Lenin for Gumilev's life, and there is even a tradition that
Lenin sent a telegram rescinding the order of execution, but
that it arrived too late. The main authority for these traditions
is Evgeny Zamyatin's memoir *Litsa* (Faces),[33] but Nadezhda
Mandelstam firmly denies their truth.[34]

During the approximately three weeks from arrest to execution, none of Gumilev's family, friends, or associates were allowed to communicate with him, although some of his students
took a package to the prison for him daily and he was permitted
to send at least one letter out to his wife ("Don't worry. I am
well; I'm writing poetry and playing chess").[35] Thus we have
no direct reports of those three weeks. There are second- and
third-hand descriptions of the interrogations and execution.
These may not be accurate in all details, but there is no reason
to doubt their general import: that Gumilev faced his inter-
rogators and executioners with unbending dignity and unflinching courage.

We have little information regarding Gumilev's participation
in the Tagantsev conspiracy, so called after its organizer. It
has even been suggested that he was innocent of any counterrevolutionary activities,[36] but Odoevtseva's memoirs, if accurate,
leave no doubt on this score. (By the way, some details of her
account coincide with the text of the above-mentioned newspaper notice, which states that Gumilev "actively participated
in the writing of a counterrevolutionary proclamation, prom-

ised in the event of an uprising to bring into contact with the organization a group of intellectuals who would take an active part in the uprising, received money from the organization for technical purposes.")[37] More common in the memoir literature is the suggestion that he was not a serious conspirator, that his activity was a frivolous flirting with danger for the sake of thrills and the gratification of a heroic self-image. Such innuendos, while they may contain a grain of truth, are grossly unfair to Gumilev, for his participation in the conspiracy was probably a serious and considered action, the consequence of an opposition to the regime based on deep and firm convictions. The precise nature of those convictions, though, is difficult to define. He was not a political creature, and there is no evidence that he was involved in any political activities or groupings from his boyhood flirtation with Marxism—if that report is not spurious—to the Tagantsev conspiracy. He apparently spoke very little about his political views. To be sure, he was known to state, quite openly, that he was a monarchist, and various memoirists have spoken of him as a deeply religious person.[38] Of course, those two beliefs provided more than ample grounds for antipathy toward the Bolshevik regime, yet it would be an oversimplification of Gumilev's motivations to draw the conclusion that he joined the conspiracy in order to defend the Church and restore the throne. The really central conviction, the driving force that made him translate his antipathy into direct action, was his conception of his role and his duty as a poet. Gumilev considered poetry the highest sphere of human endeavor and the poet the highest type of human being, and believed that, to be worthy of the title of poet, a man had to translate his beliefs into action, whatever the obstacles and dangers; to express his will; and insofar as possible to impose his will on the world. In other words, his counterrevolutionary activity was the ultimate expression of that principle that shaped his life and informed so much of his poetry, what one critic has called the "pathos of endeavor" (*pafos stremleniia*).[39]

Olga Forsh, an author not especially close to Gumilev on either the personal or literary plane, evokes the shock of the news of Gumilev's execution:

The next day, although the streets were filled with people, they seemed deserted. Such a silence can be found only in the steppe at burning noon, or when there is a deceased person in a house and the living have just entered his room. A sentence, already carried out, was pasted on the posts. The poet's name appeared there. No one explained anything to anyone. No one asked for explanations. There was no crush around the notices. A new person would come up to those already standing there motionless, would read it—and would move away a little and remain standing. On the avenues, streets and squares, people turned to stone. A stone city.[40]

Shortly after Gumilev's death, the collection of verse that he had already prepared for the press was published, but he or someone else had changed the title from *In the Middle of the Journey of Life* to *Ognennyi stolp* (Pillar of Fire). Three years later, the famous historian of Russian literature Dmitry Mirsky wrote: "He died at the height of his powers (nel mezzo del commin [*sic*]—35 years old), when he had just given us his best book (*Pillar of Fire*)—a tremendous step forward, which opened up unexpected horizons for his poetry."[41] This statement is one of the very few judgments on Gumilev's poetry that have never been a matter of dispute: everyone agrees that his last book is his best, and that it gives promise of still greater achievements, had he lived longer. And for this reason, his untimely death was a tragedy for Russian literature, as well as a personal tragedy. However, it allowed him to share the fate of some of Russia's finest poets, who also died unnatural deaths before their full potential was achieved: Pushkin, Lermontov, Griboedov, Esenin, Mayakovsky, Mandelstam.

When Achilles was given the choice between a long but ordinary and uneventful life, and a short but glorious one, he chose the latter. Gumilev, in a sense, made an even more courageous choice, for he was already in the midst of a brilliant career, and had every reason to expect even greater success and fame, yet he risked these, together with the life he had such an appetite for, in upholding his own ideal of what a man and a poet should be.

The years 1922 and 1923 saw a whole series of publications of Gumilev, both previously unpublished material and new editions of material published in his lifetime. The first category consisted of: *Stikhotvoreniia. Posmertnyi sbornik* (Poems. A Post-humous Collection, 1922), edited by Georgy Ivanov; a second, augmented edition appeared in 1923; *To a Blue Star;* and some of his translations. In the second category there were: second editions of *The Quiver, The Pyre, Pillar of Fire, The Porcelain Pavilion, Mik,* and *The Child of Allah;* a collection of short stories entitled *Ten' ot pal'my* (Palm Tree Shade, 1922), works written between 1907 and 1919, most of which appeared previously in periodicals, but some were apparently published for the first time here; and a collection of his critical articles under the title *Pis'ma o russkoi poezii* (Letters on Russian Poetry, 1923). All the articles had appeared in periodicals, but not all of them under that heading in *Apollon.*

This brief outburst of publications was but the prelude, as it turned out, to the virtually complete disappearance of Gumilev's poetry from the Soviet press, for in the fifty years from 1923 to the present, his poetry has been published only *three* times in the USSR, to my knowledge. In 1942, a small selection of his poetry was published in a tiny edition of but 500 copies in Odessa; in 1962, an anthology of the poetry of the early twentieth century included eight of his poems;[42] and in 1967 *Literaturnaya gazeta* (Literary Gazette) carried a single Gumilev poem. Besides these, a few more poems and parts of poems have crept into print in the form of quotations in articles and books, but from about the mid-1920s on, even the mention of his name, let alone quotations from his poetry, has been rare. It is a depressing manifestation of state control over culture that such a major poet could be virtually purged from the official annals of a national literature. At the same time, it is an indication of the limits on that control, as well as a tribute to the good sense and literary intelligence of the educated Soviet reading public, that Gumilev's poetry still lives in the Soviet Union, despite the best efforts of the official literary apparatus. Even though, for all practical purposes, he has not been printed in the USSR for fifty years, I have met Soviet citizens of a variety of professions who, on learning that I was interested in Gumilev, quoted his poetry to me by heart. Others have had similar experiences.

The Russian literary emigration has of course also kept Gumilev's name alive over the past half-century, through memoirs, tributes, and occasional editions of his poetry, but technical and financial difficulties made a really satisfactory edition of his work impossible until relatively recently, when this serious gap was filled by the four-volume *Collected Works of N. Gumilev*, published by Victor Kamkin between 1962 and 1968, and edited by Gleb Struve and Boris Filippov. This edition, for which we owe the editors and publishers a tremendous debt of gratitude, is both scholarly and as complete as humanly possible, under the circumstances. At the end of the introductory essay to Volume I (1962), Professor Struve cited some of the indications that the ban on Gumilev's name in the USSR might finally be lifted in the near future. To date, more than fifteen years later, these promises have not been fulfilled. But given the growing interest, both in and out of the Soviet Union, in that amazing period in Russian literary history known as the Silver Age, of which Gumilev is such an important part, we may still hope that they soon will be, and that Nikolay Gumilev will at last be given a measure of official recognition at least somewhat more in accord with his real stature and importance in the poetry of Russia.

CHAPTER 2

The Early Poetry (1903–1910)

I The Path of Conquistadors

THERE is not much that can be said at this point about Gumilev's earliest development as a poet. Despite their best efforts, the editors of the recent four-volume edition of Gumilev were able to unearth only one poem predating his first collection of poems: the 1902 lyric "Ia v les bezhal iz gorodov" (I fled the cities for the woods, II, 121–22). The poem has no intrinsic artistic significance, but for the student of Gumilev's poetry, it is of some interest for its echoes of Lermontov, in particular the Romantic conflict between human failings and the thirst for the ideal. Gumilev was a Romantic idealist and an admirer of Lermontov all his life, facts which have been somewhat obscured by his reputation as the leader of Acmeism, supposedly a neo-Classical school oriented toward Pushkin.

In the immediate sequel, however, the influence of Lermontov was temporarily obscured by that of a modern version of Romanticism: Symbolism, the dominant school in Russian poetry from about 1895 to about 1910. Valery Bryusov, himself a leader of the Russian Symbolists, emphasized this influence in his review of *The Path of Conquistadors*: "In his choice of themes, in his manner of writing (*po priemam tvorchestva*), the author obviously belongs to 'the new school' in poetry. But so far his verses are only echoes and imitations. . . . In this book are re-iterated all the usual precepts of Decadence that astonished the public by their boldness and novelty about twenty years ago in the West, and about ten years ago here. . . . Individual stanzas are painfully reminiscent of their models: now Balmont, now Andrey Bely, now A. Blok."[1] What Bryusov mainly stresses in this brief review is not so much the fact of influence *per se* as its uncreative assimilation; that is, the highly imitative and

47

derivative nature of the poetry. The accusation is just. *The Path* shows that Gumilev had read modern poetry and absorbed its themes, moods, and images, and had gained sufficient control of the techniques of verse-writing to be able to reproduce and recombine those images and themes in reasonably smooth and polished verse. But with occasional exceptions these verses create the impression that the influence has been transmitted from the author's brain to his pen hand without passing through his heart; they do not seem to convey any felt experience, but to be more or less mechanical exercises on fashionable themes. Gumilev himself later regarded the book as the mere incunabula of his work, and regretted having published it. He told Odoevtseva that he bought up as many copies as he could and burned them, much as Gogol had done with his first work long before. He did what he could to expunge the book from his canon: the title page of *Foreign Skies,* his fourth book (including *The Path*), carried the designation "Third book of verses," and when he began in 1918 to publish revised editions of his earlier collections, he started with *Romantic Flowers* and continued in chronological order, ignoring, as it were, the existence of *The Path*.

The major influences perceptible in the book are the first two of those Bryusov mentioned: Konstantin Balmont and Andrey Bely. Balmont's influence is obvious in such poems as "Osen' " (Autumn) and "Kogda iz temnoi bezdny zhizni" (When, from the dark abyss of life), with their themes of spiritual and physical metamorphoses (the theme of the poet as Proteus is one of Balmont's favorites), or in "Rusalka" (The Mermaid), with its unusual rhyme scheme, anapestic meter, and insistent sound effects:

> Na rusalke gorit ozherel'e
> I rubiny grekhovno-krasny,
> Eto stranno-pechal'nye sny
> Mirovogo, bol'nogo pokhmel'ia.
> Na rusalke gorit ozherel'e
> I rubiny grekhovno-krasny.   (I, 37)

> The mermaid wears a blazing necklace,
> And its rubies are sin-red:

They are the strangely-sad dreams
That follow a cosmic, morbid intoxication.
The mermaid wears a blazing necklace,
And its rubies are sin-red.

But still more obvious, the most insistent presence in the book as a whole is the influence of Bely: the leading images, the color scheme, the vocabulary and diction of many of the poems, especially the longer ones, are derived directly from Bely. Bely's first book of poems was entitled *Zoloto v lazuri* (Gold in Azure, 1904), and the gorgeous coloration of that book cast its refulgence over Gumilev's early poetry, which is replete with color, especially golds, blues, reds, and whites. Many of the personae of *The Path*'s poems—the kings and queens, knights and maidens, gnomes, sibyls, driads, and hunchbacks—come from *Gold in Azure* and from Bely's first prose-poem, *Severnaia simfoniia* (The Northern Symphony), and perhaps also directly from the Nordic mythology and contemporary Scandinavian poets that were Bely's main sources. The same is true of the settings and paraphernalia: the snow-covered mountain peaks, showing white against an azure sky, or dyed crimson by a resplendent sunset; the marble palaces, marble temples, and marble grottos; the gold and precious stones; the mantles and crowns; swords and armor; harps.

As Bryusov indicated, some phrases and lines are lifted bodily out of Bely. For example, the phrase "intoxicating crimsons" (of sunsets) (*p'ianiashchie bagriantsy*) in "Skazka o Koroliakh" (Tale of the Kings) is taken from Bely's "The flamelets of heaven's candles" (*Ogonechki nebesnykh svechei*), part of a cycle "To Balmont." Similarly, the line "With the blue happiness of sorrow" (*Golubeiushchim schast'em pechali*), also in "Tale of the Kings," recalls some lines from the same cycle by Bely: "Your blue ecstasies" (*Golubye vostorgi tvoi*) and "Of laughing melancholy" (*O smeiushcheisia grusti*), and rhythmically, *"Golubeiushchii barkhat efira"* (The blue velvet of the ether). But while Bely's separate expressions are effective enough in their contexts, Gumilev's attempt to merge them does not come off poetically. The image, like so many of the images in his early poetry, obscures rather than sharpens meaning, and the combination of synaesthesia and oxymoron in a single line is stylistically too Baroque for the context.

The influences of Balmont and Bely were primarily a matter of externals. It is harder to attribute the substance of the poems in *The Path* to specific influences. They echo then-fashionable ideas and themes—the search for the ideal, the transcendence of the earthly, the conflict between passion and spirituality, the struggle of the individualist as poet, prophet, aesthete, "conquistador"—but they do so in a generalized, diffuse, and eclectic manner that blurs possible specific resemblances. There is, however, one clear and acknowledged ideological influence: that of Nietzsche, whose ideas, or rather attitudes, had a permanent and in part pernicious effect on Gumilev.[2] But it is only in the early poetry that Gumilev directly echoes undigested Nietzschean themes, as in "Pesn' Zaratustry" (The Song of Zarathustra, I, 5–6):

> Oh, young, bright brethren
> Of strength, ecstasy, and dream,
> To you I open my embrace,
> I, the son of the blue heights.
>
> . . . .
>
> The poet's ardent heart
> Glitters, like sounding steel.
> Woe to them who know not the light!
> Woe to them who embrace sorrow!

or in "Inogda ia byvaiu pechalen" (I am sometimes sorrowful, I, 40–41):

> If you want to unfold bright horizons
> Before the ailing people,
> Then take into your mighty heart
> Days of silent, burning grief.

The Path of Conquistadors is a small volume, consisting of sixteen lyrics and three longer poems, less than a thousand lines in all. The book carries an epigraph from André Gide, and opens with an introductory sonnet from which the book title derives:

"I am a conquistador in iron armor." The rest is divided into three sections, each with its own heading and epigraph. The first section, consisting of six short lyrics, is called "Mechi i potselui" (Swords and Kisses); the epigraph reads "I know that we are given nights of love, / And bright hot days for war." These two lines are signed "N. Gumilev," but do not appear in any known Gumilev poem, so that they were either composed just for this epigraph, or taken from an unpublished or still undiscovered poem. The second section is entitled simply "Poemy"—(the Russian term for longer, narrative poems)—and the epigraph, "We will wrest the truth from God / With the force of flaming swords," is taken from one of the three poems in that section. The third section, containing nine short lyrics, is headed "Vysoty i bezdny" (Summits and Abysses), and its epigraph, "Who knows the dark depths of the human soul, / Its ecstasies and its sorrows?! / They are tablets, concealed from us / By a blue enamel," is likewise from one of the poems of the second section.

All these headings and inbred epigraphs sound almost unbearably pretentious when quoted out of context, and it must be admitted that there is a good deal of pretentiousness about the book—the pretensions to esoteric profundity of the Age of Symbolism added to the natural pretensions of youth. The only thing that somewhat redeems it all is a certain air of naive honesty—the impression that the poet has not just hopped on to the bandwagon of literary fashion, but really believes in the significance and worth of all this nonsense, and therefore has managed to put some small part of himself into it, despite his use of all the ready-made images and formulas and trappings and themes. For there is, after all, a faint but perceptible note of individuality in the book, beneath all the imitation; as the critic Yury Verkhovsky wrote, *The Path* is one of those first books in which one can just begin to see the outlines of "certain elements of the [poet's] future distinctive development."[3] They are seen in most concentrated form in the opening sonnet:

> I am a conquistador in iron armor,
> I gaily follow my star,
> I pass along precipices and abysses
> And rest in a gladsome garden.

How troubled is the wild and starless sky!
A mist rises . . . but I wait in silence,
And I believe that I will find my love . . .
I am a conquistador in iron armor.

And if there's nothing that day can tell the stars,
Then I myself will create my own dream
And will spellbind it with the song of battles.

I am forever a brother to precipices and storms,
But into my martial array I'll plait
The star of the valleys, a sky-blue lily.   (I, 3)

Not a terribly compelling piece of poetry, to be sure, but characteristic in a number of ways. For one thing, it illustrates the propensities for the decorative image and the rhetorical tone that marred so much of Gumilev's poetry until he began to learn to control them, rather than they him. Further, we see concentrated here a number of the central themes of Gumilev's subsequent poetry: the spirit of adventure, accompanied by aestheticism ("I pass along precipices and abysses, / And rest in a gladsome garden": The garden is a recurrent image in Gumilev's early poetry, an emblem of physical beauty and spiritual harmony); the buoyant and self-confident optimism ("I gaily follow my star," "And I believe that I will find my love," "Then I myself will create my own dream"); and the Romantic quest for the Ideal, and for the ideal love (the lines just quoted; note also the Novalislike image of the last line, which juxtaposes two of Gumilev's favorite metaphors for ideal love, especially but not only in his early poetry—the star and the flower, the latter usually white rather than blue). These themes are central ones from the beginning to the end of Gumilev's poetic career because they reflect basic elements of his personality. But they are not the only major themes, for that personality was a complex and often contradictory one: for example, alongside the moods of optimism are often found notes of disillusionment and resignation.

The three long poems of the book's middle section are a fairly ambitious attempt at the sort of "myth-making" that was popular in the Symbolist period. A brief description of them may give the reader a fuller idea of the nature and atmosphere of Gumilev's earliest poetry.

"Deva Solntsa" (The Sun-Maiden, I, 13–17) consists of thirty quatrains of iambic tetrameter. A "mighty tsar" recalls the dream visions he had in his youth of the Sun Maiden, and sends his slaves out to find her and bring her to him. He waits for many months, and finally messengers arrive with news that the "holy maiden" is nearing the city walls. He rushes to meet her, but she passes by, silent, and he drowns his sorrow in blood: "He is like a tempest, he proudly deals destruction / In the flaming sunset of a dream, / Because he loves excessively / The extravagantly white flowers" (I, 17). The flowers had been introduced earlier as an attribute of the maiden, one of several attributes and epithets calculated to suggest without saying it that she is the embodiment of purity, compassion, and virtue. By the way, the flowers' epithet, "extravagantly white" (*bezumnobelye*) is a typical example of the compound-color adjectives, not always very intelligible, that Gumilev uses frequently in his early poetry, following another current fashion and Bely in particular. Power and violence, then, fail in the attempt to regain youthful innocence, and in frustration become still more violent. But the poem closes on a pseudophilosophical note that attempts to reconcile the conflicting forces on a higher level: "But the world is sunk in strict silence, / It knows the truth, it knows the dreams, / And death and Blood are given us by God / In order to set off Whiteness."

"Osenniaia pesnia" (Autumn Song I, 17–26) is also in iambic tetrameter quatrains and is nearly twice as long (216 lines) as "The Sun Maiden." We are shown a marble temple in a forest. Sometimes at night, a young dryad visits the temple—stealthily, for "Children of sin and sensuality / May not be in that temple" —and flings on the floor a purple rose that glows through the night and dies at dawn. And at sunset, a woman kneels at the temple altar. A voice comes, telling her she is not yet ready for the refuge of the "Joyful God," because she is still in the power of earthly forces, she still finds enjoyment in the night, where her sister the dryad lives, "And you still so love the laughter / Of the earthly, scarlet cloak, / And you plait bright sin / Into the garlands of blue heaven." If she desires the world of Day, she

must surrender up her sister the dryad to the flames, "And let
her be consumed within you ... When you abandon the joy of
the forests, / You will become divinely free." There follows the
dryad's bridal song to her fiancé the "Prince of Fire," in a different
meter, and a description of their "wedding," then a description
of the transfiguration of the woman: "And, invested in the
fabric of the sun,[4] / She is a great holy person, / No longer
a pale woman, / But a sovereign goddess." But apparently her
transfiguration is also the transfiguration of the world: cosmic
waves roll through the ether, the White Child (*Beloe Ditia*)
celebrates a liturgy, and "The White Rider sounded the call ...
That the moment had come, the great moment ... And the dryad,
the dream of earth, is no more / Before the bright hour of
awakening."

The third long poem, "Tale of the Kings" (I, 26–33), is about
midway in length between the other two (172 lines). The meter
changes several times in the course of the poem: sections in
trochaic tetrameter alternate with sections in anapests. The
narrative structure is very loose; the poem consists essentially
of a series of loosely connected vignettes, most of them centered
around the speech of one of the characters; the changes in
meter generally parallel the boundaries between "scenes." After
three kings have spoken in turn regarding what kind of path
they should try to follow to the Ideal, the group of kings decides
that the secrets of the universe may be discovered through
forceful action:

> The path to the Unknown Bride
> Is our only sure path
>
> . . . .
>
> The World Maiden (*Deva Mira*) will be ours,
> Ours she must be!
>
> Let us wrench from the tablet of joy
> The grey, pallid shroud,
> And the distances that open out
> Will tell us the truth of dreams.
>
> This is the sure road,
> The world is either ours, or no one's,

> We will wrest the truth from God
> With the force of flaming swords.   (I, 30)

They don their armor and set out, and they meet the Earth-Maiden (*Deva Zemli*), as she is called this time, but fail to win her love, and they all perish in battle.

The thematic links that interconnect the three poems indicate the directions of Gumilev's poetic thought at this stage. All three involve a feminine being who represents some sort of ideal; in the first and third poems she is sought after by kings, but rejects them, and the poems end on a negative, pessimistic note. Otherwise, the first two are more closely related, and the third stands somewhat apart. Both "The Sun-Maiden" and "Autumn Song" have to do with a conflict between purity and passions (in the former, the passions of power and violence; in the latter, sensuality), and extensive use is made of color symbolism in both: various shades of red, associated mainly with the tsar of "The Sun-Maiden" and the dryad of "Autumn Song," are contrasted to white, light blue, and to some extent gold, associated with the Sun-Maiden and the woman. There are also important differences between the two. In the second poem purity triumphs over passion, while in the first there is, strictly, no conflict, for the two simply cannot be reconciled and each goes its separate way. In both poems, the two principles are embodied in separate personae, but in "Autumn Song" the dryad and the woman are quite clearly meant as alter egos, two aspects of the same person, while in "The Sun-Maiden," they seem to be separate, although one could possibly see the Sun-Maiden as no more than a personification of the tsar's fitful yearnings for youthful innocence.

In the "Tale of the Kings," the conflict is a different one: between two approaches to the ideal: that of withdrawal, transcendentalism; and that of action ("We will wrest the truth from God"). The conflict is not developed through dramatic action as in the other two poems, but simply presented in the speeches of the kings, and if the failure of their expedition is meant to imply the superiority of the passive path, this by no means is made clear. The color symbolism of the other two poems is virtually absent.

These poems, of course, take place in a realm of absolute fantasy, and this is a feature that extends to the rest of the poetry in the book. There is not a single earthly landscape; all of the characters are creatures of the imagination. Even in the first-person lyrics, the persona is not, except in a very indirect psychological sense, Nikolay Gumilev, young nobleman in turn-of-the-century Russia, but a conquistador, a king, a prophet, a ghost, or simply an unidentifiable aesthete. The result is a level of poetic abstraction that may sustain an individual poem, but not an entire collection, and on the whole *The Path of Conquistadors* is rather like cotton candy, pleasant enough when one is in the mood for it, but insubstantial. It is insubstantial not only because the poetic world itself is chimerical, but also because the imagination that created it was not the poet's own, and therefore that world lacks individuality; it lacks the weight that a specific creative personality lends to a body of poetry. The main process of development of Gumilev's poetry over the next several years is its gradual acquisition of body and weight, both through the introduction of more mundane settings, and through the emergence of a more definite poetic personality. To be sure, Gumilev will appear before us in his poetry behind a mask for a long time, almost to the end, but it will be a mask of his own manufacture, as opposed to the set of borrowed masks of his earliest poetry.

II Romantic Flowers

Three years after *The Path of Conquistadors*, Gumilev published *Romantic Flowers* (Paris, 1908). Meanwhile, he had published a number of poems in various periodicals, including several in Bryusov's very prestigious *Vesy* (The Scales). *Romantic Flowers*, in this first edition,[5] was an even more slender volume than *The Path*: it contained thirty-two poems, most of them short, totaling less than 750 lines.

The versification of this book, like that of *The Path*, is conventional. Nearly all the poems are in standard syllabo-tonic meters; only two are in the accentual versification that was becoming firmly established in Russian poetry in the early part of this century.

Bryusov's review of *Romantic Flowers*, as noted above, was

considerably more positive than his review of *The Path*: "the author has worked diligently at his verse. There is not a trace left of the former metrical carelessness, the slovenly rhymes, the inaccuracy of images. N. Gumilev's verses are now attractive, graceful, and for the most part formally *interesting;* now he delineates his images sharply and clearly, and chooses his epithets with greater care and refinement."[6] To be sure he had reservations ("Of course ... *Romantic Flowers* is only the book of an apprentice"), but Bryusov correctly guessed that Gumilev was one of those writers "who develop slowly, and for that very reason reach a high level of attainment."

This time, Bryusov was not the only important critic to review the book, and Gumilev must have been at least as pleased by the slightly ironic but penetrating and basically sympathetic analysis of the book by his former teacher, Annensky, as he was by Bryusov's reserved and somewhat superficial praise. Annensky's review[7] emphasizes the decadent, "Parisian" artificiality of the book's exoticism: "There is no Ancient East here, nor any millennial mist; the whole setting for this 'Assyrian romance' is—the boulevard, a bec Auer [gas lamp—E.S.], and a stretch of rain-wet pavement in front of a café." That was not intended to be as critical as it probably sounds out of context. Annensky's own poetry, after all, was in its own way artificial and decadent, being no doubt among the finest decadent poetry ever written, as most of the poetry of the age was, and in Annensky's view had to be: "And I am glad that the romantic flowers are artificial, for the poetry of live flowers is long since dead. And will it ever be reborn?" Throughout the review, the infinitely subtle Annensky maintains an ambiguously ironic tone that not so much alternates between praise and criticism as merges the two. Even the final paragraph, traditionally reserved in reviews of young writers for the note of encouragement, maintains this balance: "Gumilev follows sensitively the rhythms of his impressions and is able to subordinate his lyricism to his artistic intention [ironic, surely, since this is the one thing young Gumilev not only "is able" to do, but does with a vitiating vengeance—E.S.], and besides, and this is especially important, he loves culture and is not afraid of the bourgeois aftertaste of beauty."

The improvement in technique that Bryusov noted is not all that makes *Romantic Flowers* a better book than *The Path*. To be sure, it is still, in Bryusov's words, "the book of an apprentice." In fact, it is in a way more truly the book of an apprentice than *The Path*. In the earlier book, Gumilev imitated everybody, and therefore nobody; in *Flowers* he has apprenticed himself to a particular master—Valery Bryusov. Not that other influences could not be discovered in the book if one so desired,[8] but it has far more of a unity, a specific tonality, than did *The Path*. Gumilev has chosen for his master the one among his immediate elders whose artistic sensibility is closest to his own, and since an artist reveals himself in his affinities and sympathies as well as in his inventions, this in itself is a step toward individuality. In *The Path*, he had not even advanced far enough along "the path" of self-realization to make such a choice. In *Flowers*, he has come that far, and then some, for his dependence on Bryusov is less direct, less slavish than was his dependence on his various earlier models. He has advanced from imitation to more creative assimilation of influence. His imagination, which manifested itself clearly enough in his first book, is here freer, so that one review could speak of "a well-developed artistic imagination, and a certain originality, a literary independence, which allow the young poet to devise for himself a whole world of creative fantasies, in which he rather skillfully lives and rules."[9]

By the time Gumilev's second book appeared, there was a fairly clear split in the Symbolists' ranks between the "aesthetes" —those who regarded Symbolism primarily as a literary technique —and the "mystics"—those who regarded it as an instrument of revelation, prophecy, theurgy, even transfiguration. Bryusov was the leader of the aesthetes, Blok the main figure among the mystics. Bryusov was always more interested in problems of form, in aesthetic issues, than in metaphysics, and when he almost singlehandedly introduced French Symbolism into Russia in the 1890s, he was more concerned with the "physical" renewal of debile Russian verse through the new expressive possibilities of symbolistic technique than with transcendentalities. He was also wary of the extreme subjectivism of the mystical Symbolists, and as he grew older his verse moved in the direction of a more "objective" style, a style less dependent on the evocative effects of atmosphere and verse music than on visual and plastic imagery, a style less confessional than what might be called emblematic; i.e., a style in which the lyric "I" does not reveal itself directly, but indirectly, through third-person personae. Thus one of Bryusov's favorite genres was the historical or mythological ballad, a Schilleresque use of material from existing traditions as the basis for short narrative pieces. The literary scholar Renato Poggioli sums up this development in terms of influences: "While Bryusov's earlier books had been primarily influenced by . . . Baudelaire, Mallarmé, and especially Maeterlinck, the poetry of his maturity found its formal ideals in Gautier, the Parnassians, and even in Pushkin. . . ."[10]

These, then, are the qualities in Bryusov that attracted Gumilev: his interest in poetic form, his avoidance of the higher realms of metaphysics, and the relative objectivity of his style. Bryusov himself, in his review, emphasized the latter element: "N. Gumilev is most successful in 'objective' lyrics, where the poet disappears behind the images he has drawn, where more is given to the eye than the ear. . . . He is something of a Parnassian, . . . a poet of the type of Leconte de Lisle. Diffident in his personal feelings, he avoids speaking in the first person . . . and prefers to hide behind the mask of one hero or another. He is also close to the Parnassians in his love for exotic images. . . ."[11] Bryusov is no doubt right that Gumilev had read, admired, and wanted to imitate the Parnassians; he is silent, perhaps out of conventional modesty, about his own more substantial influence. He also defines accurately the major point of difference between the Parnassians and Gumilev (and himself): "But N. Gumilev is less restrained than were most of the Parnassians, and the pictures his fantasy sketches for us are . . . bold and unexpected."

Like his master, Gumilev turns rather often to the genre of "little ballad," a short narrative, usually third-person. Verkhovsky explains the preference for this form in terms of stylistic traits: ". . . a predilection for colorful and plastic motifs and a decorative treatment of them; hence an objectification, a projection of the personal element outward, and thus a preference for lyro-epic forms, for the conventional ballad style (uslovnoballadnogo sklada).[12] *Flowers* includes such ballads on a variety of sub-

jects: fairy-tale ("Printsessa" [The Princess], "Vliublennaia v
D'iavola" [In Love with the Devil], "Neoromanticheskaia skazka"
[Neo-Romantic Fairy-Tale]); ancient Roman ("Pompei u piratov"
[Pompey Among the Pirates], "Osnovateli" [The Founders], "Igry"
[The Games], "Caracalla"); African ("Ozero Chad" [Lake
Chad]); fantasy or dream-ballads ("Peshchera sna" [The Cave of
Dream], "Uzhas" [Terror]), etc.

One of the most striking differences between *The Path* and
Flowers is the greater palpability of the poetic world in the
new book, which is partly but not entirely the result of Gumilev's
imitation of Bryusov's pseudohistorical ballads and the Parnassians' descriptions of exotic regions. Thus, while Gumilev is
not primarily concerned with historical accuracy in his Roman
poems,[13] or with descriptive realism in his African poems, but
rather with a certain mood and atmosphere in each case, still
the specificity of historical or geographical setting gives them a
concreteness, a relative "reality" that none of the poems of *The
Path* has. Furthermore, there are a few poems in the book
whose setting is neither fantastic nor exotic, poems such as
"Perchatka" (The Glove), "Samoubiistvo" (The Suicide), "Krest"
(The Cross), and "Krysa" (The Rat), which take place in the
world of everyday reality. Such poems are a sign of the young
poet's growing confidence. He is now willing, even if only
occasionally, to cast aside the crutches of gaudily fantastic or
exotic themes and settings, and the stylized, "gorgeous" diction
and imagery that goes with them, and to depend for his poetic
effect on his skill in the choice and disposition of more ordinary
words and images.

The majority of the poems in the book, to be sure, are set in
the same realms of fantasy as *The Path*. But many of these are
considerably more substantial in texture, more down-to-earth,
than the poems of the earlier book. For example, "The Princess,"
which tells of a young princess who loses her way in the forest
and is sheltered for the night by a forester in his hut, includes
such lines as these:

> He led her to his hut,
> Gave her a biscuit with bitter suet,

> Put a pillow under her head
> And covered her legs with a blanket.
>
> ....
>
> Are these really only rags,
> Pitiful, useless refuse,
> Dried rabbits-feet,
> Cigarettes thrown on the floor?   (I, 62)

Of course, in a work of imaginative literature, there can be no sharp distinction between the realm of fantasy and the realm of reality. Take, for example, a poem like "Otkaz" (The Rejection, I, 56–57). An empress (*tsaritsa*) stands on the seashore. Dolphins appear and offer her their backs, to ride to the "domains of a prince in love with her," but she refuses. On the "plot" level, this poem has nothing to do with everyday reality. But on another level it may be read as a transformation into highly fanciful imagistic terms of a quite "real" rejection of a lover's suit. There is in fact a rather clear hint of this in the first line, repeated with a change of one word as the next-to-last line: "An empress—or, perhaps, merely a sorrowful [penultimate line: capricious] child."

A more definite linking of the two realms occurs in some poems in which the fantasy is more or less explicitly justified as a dream or the product of the imagination. For example, the poem "Iaguar" (The Jaguar), in which the rejected lover is a jaguar brought to bay by the merciless lady's dogs, begins with the line "I had a strange dream last night." In "The Cave of Dreams" the title is the only direct indication that the fantastic figures in the poem are dream-images, but there is a hint in the text itself, as the poem begins with nightfall and ends with sunrise.[14] "Korabl'" (The Ship) portrays a ship scudding over the sea, and an empress, again, standing on a seaside cliff and beckoning it to its destruction. As in "The Rejection," this scene is a fanciful image for the relationship between the lady and her would-be lover or lovers. But in this case the emblematic significance of the scene is more directly revealed: the poem opens with the lady's quoted question, "What do you see in my eyes?", followed by the poet's answer, "I see in them the deep sea / And a great sunken ship" (I, 68). The rest of the poem expands that image.

Associated with this willingness to plot more precisely the correspondences between the real world and the world of the poetic imagination is a more precise use of imagery. By making the imagined worlds of the poems of *The Path*—and some of those in *Flowers*—apparently autonomous, Gumilev tended to leave his images floating vaguely around a cluster or over a range of possible meanings, or to give them quite generalized allegorical meanings as he did especially in the long poems of *The Path*, whereas in *Flowers* the meaning of images tends on the whole to be more specific; e.g., jaguar = rejected lover; sunken ship = broken heart, etc.

The thematics of *Romantic Flowers* are likewise somewhat more specific than those of *The Path*. In general terms, the main themes are much the same: love, death, passion vs. purity, etc. But while *The Path* tended to treat these themes broadly, vaguely, metaphysically, allegorically, the poems of *Flowers* turn rather sharply away from metaphysics and tend to isolate more specific aspects of the themes, more specific psychological or emotional situations.

The two most important themes in the book are love and death. In the spirit of the age, the two are very often linked, as in "Mne snilos'" (I Dreamed), where death brings peace and eternal union to the lovers by removing desire:

> I dreamed that we both had died,
> And were lying with calm gaze;
> Two white, white coffins
> Placed side by side
> . . . .
>
> But strange: the heart felt no pain,
> The heart didn't cry.
> . . . .
>
> And your lips aroused no desire,
> Though eternally beautiful. (I, 59)

The more interesting treatments of the theme of death, though, are those that do not juxtapose it with love, as, for example "Smert'" (Death), which contrasts two images of death as a female being (the Russian word for death is of feminine gender). The majestic image of death in battle contrasts with a tender and pale image, presumably of death by illness:

> Tender, pale, in ash-grey dress,
> You appeared to me with caressing eyes.
> Not thus did I meet you formerly,
> 'Midst the cry of trumpets and the clash of arms. (I, 50)

More in accord with the image of himself that Gumilev cultivated is the attitude toward death expressed in "Vybor" (The Choice):[15]

> The builder of towers will fall,
> Terrible will be his headlong flight,
> And, at the bottom of the cosmic well,
> He will curse his own madness,
>
> The destroyer will be crushed,
> Toppled by fragments of slabs,
> And, abandoned by the All-Seeing God,
> He will cry out his pain.
>
> And he who goes off into the caves of night
> Or to the backwaters of a quiet river
> Will meet the terrifying eyes
> Of a ferocious panther.
>
> You can't escape the bloody lot
> That Heaven has assigned to mortals.
> But be still: it's an incomparable right
> To choose oneself one's death. (I, 55)

The obvious point of the poem is given directly in the last stanza, but the unspoken implication of the first three stanzas is that it is only the doers, the bold men of action, whatever the nature of the action, who exercise that "incomparable right." A great deal of Gumilev's romantic philosophy is summed up in those last two lines and in a line from "Sady dushi" (The Gardens of the Soul): "My dreams follow only the eternal" (*Moi mechty lish' vechnomu pokorny;* I, 74).

III Pearls

By the time his third book, *Pearls,* appeared in 1910, Gumilev was well known in Petersburg literary circles, and his name was becoming familiar to a wider reading public. In 1908–10, his poems were published in the Moscow journal *Vesy,* in the newly founded journal *Apollon,* and in several lesser periodicals; in 1908 he made his first appearance in Peter Struve's *Russkaya mysl,* which had a greater circulation and a broader readership than the purely literary-artistic journals *Apollon* and *Vesy.*

Pearls was a more substantial book than the first two. In its first edition it contained eighty-seven poems and almost 2400 lines. To be sure, twenty of these were poems previously published in *Romantic Flowers,* but even without those, it was about twice as big as the earlier books. It was divided into four sections, labeled "Black Pearl," "Grey Pearl," "Pink Pearl," and "Romantic Flowers," each section with its own epigraph, from Alfred de Vigny, Bryusov, Vyacheslav Ivanov, and Annensky, respectively. The color adjectives reflect the dominant emotional tonality of each section. In "Black Pearl" moods of gloom, despair, and horror predominate; the moods of "Grey Pearl" are somewhat more neutral, but tend to ennui and resignation; and most of the book's few poems in a lighter tone or a major key are in "Pink Pearl."[16]

The versification of *Pearls* is conventional; only four poems are in accentual meters. There are a couple of modest metrical experiments; for example, "Tovarishch" (The Comrade). The meter here is iambic tetrameter, but in the first three lines of each quatrain, the first foot is trochaic (thus: $-\!-\ -\acute{-}\ -\acute{-}\ -\acute{-}$); the fourth line of each stanza is in regular iambs. The trochaic opening is not unusual as an occasional variation of the iambic line, but its consistent use in predetermined lines of a whole poem is something of a mild *tour de force.*

Pearls presents, essentially, a further development in the same directions as *Flowers*: improvements in poetic technique, such as greater felicity in the selection and disposition of words to maximum phonetic, rhythmic, and semantic effect, and a surer hand in the creation of imagery; a greater palpability and solidity of the poetic world and a more direct relationship between that world and "reality"; and a broader range of themes, materials, and moods. The influence of Bryusov is if anything even stronger than in *Flowers*. The first edition carried the inscription "Dedicated to my teacher Bryusov"; in 1918 this dedication was dropped, but the opening poem, "Volshebnaia skripka" (The Magic Violin), was inscribed "To Valery Bryusov." Bryusov's example was no doubt a significant factor in Gumilev's development along the lines mentioned above, from about 1905–10. For example, the greater palpability of the poetic world stems not only from a choice of less abstractly imaginary settings, but also from a greater plasticity and precision of imagery, which Gumilev learned from Bryusov, among others.

Pearls reveals Gumilev as a steadily developing poet, gradually but clearly fulfilling the promise of the best of his earlier poetry, and Bryusov's review of the book[17] reflects his appreciation of this fact—not so much through direct praise, although he ends the review with noticeably stronger and less reserved praise than he had for *Flowers*, as through the more serious and substantial tone of the article. Bryusov's phraseology and tone in his review of *Flowers*—which is about half of the length of his review of *Pearls*—was typical of the sort of thing an established poet writes about a beginner: a dry catalogue of strengths and weaknesses, and a circumspect assessment of future potential. But he begins his review of the new book with a discussion of the general trends in Russian poetry in recent years, in order to show where Gumilev fits into this pattern. This is a clear indication that he now sees Gumilev as a poet to be taken seriously, one who will carve a significant niche for himself.

The emphasis of Bryusov's review is on Gumilev's fantasy, on the purely imaginary nature of his poetic worlds. Vyacheslav Ivanov's review of *Pearls*[18] also strongly emphasizes this aspect, but also recognizes in passing the presence, or the promise, of another aspect, a poetic world more directly related to reality: "Occasionally true Reality—res intima rerum—appears like a vague summons in the poet's dreams. . . ." Ivanov's review is still more substantial than Bryusov's, more of a short critical study than a review. Bryusov's strong influence is not only mentioned, as it was in Bryusov's own review ("The pupil of I.

Annensky, of Vyacheslav Ivanov, and of the poet to whom *Pearls* is dedicated"), but substantiated at some length. He also points out differences, including the fact that Gumilev imitates Bryusov in the latter's creation of imaginary worlds, but not in his responses to the stimuli of the real world. Ivanov closes with a mention of Gumilev's tendency to allow his lyricism to be overwhelmed by the epic element—by which Ivanov presumably means both the narrative and descriptive aspects—and a prognosis that further spiritual growth will lead to a clear division and separate manifestation of the lyric and epic elements: "then his lyrical epos will become an objective epos, and his hidden lyricism—pure lyric." This prophecy is not particularly accurate: Gumilev's later poetry is characterized rather by a true equilibrium of the lyric and epic elements, an organic synthesis, than by their separation. But the prognosis is preceded by a highly expressive characterization of the general tone of *Pearls*, worth being quoted at length: "a circumscription of poetic scope, and unresponsiveness, bordering at times on naive incomprehension, to everything that lies outside the borders of his dream. . . . Unresponsiveness—and a preening, deliberately posing, solemnly retarded, pompous monotone, a lack of agility, of spontaneity, of live mobility, of live reaction to the diversity of real life. Yet there is no deficiency of lyrical energy: it moves and agitates every stanza, underneath every image beats a living heart." While the reservation should be made that this is a general statement, which would be inappropriate to a number of the individual poems in *Pearls*, it does convey very nicely the general atmosphere of Gumilev's poetry at this period. Furthermore, the contrast noted in the last two sentences is one that is present to some degree for all the remainder of Gumilev's career. There is at every period a certain tendency toward a formal monumentality, a solemnity that is sometimes impressive, sometimes merely pompous, but which is almost always underlain by a powerful intensity of lyric feeling. As the poet develops, it is more and more often the case that the lyrical intensity *determines* the style, whether solemn or otherwise, rather than being constrained and, as it were, concealed by it.

But for the time being, it is the deliberate, stylized solemnity—derived primarily, as in *Flowers,* from Bryusov's ballad style—that is the chief merit of most of the successful poems in *Pearls.* Similarly, most if not all of the flawed poems occur when the poet's control or taste betrays him in his efforts to create such a style. One example of this is the execrable line from the poem "Poedinok" (The Duel): *"Luchi, sokroitesia nazad vy,"* which can be approximately conveyed by "Oh ye rays, retreat back into darkness," meaning that the poet dreads the coming of the day. The stanza containing this line was discarded in the 1918 edition.

This solemn style is used not only in the Bryusovian "little ballads," which are still more frequent than in *Flowers* and in fact constitute most of the book, but as well in poems that are more lyric in construction and theme. *Pearls* opens with such a lyric, one of the finest in the book, "The Magic Violin" (I, 93–94). This is a symbolic poem on the fate of the poet: once he has taken up this instrument, he may never set it down again, for bloodthirsty wolves dog the musician's footsteps, and the moment the music stops, they will destroy him. The solemnity of style in this case depends to a great extent on repetitions, cast in an unusually long eight-foot trochaic line:

> Nado vechno pet' i plakat' etim strunam, zvonkim strunam,
> Vechno dolzhen bit'sia, vit'sia obezumevshii smychok,
> I pod solntsem, i pod v'iugoi, pod beleiushchim burunom,
> I kogda pylaet zapad, i kogda gorit vostok.

> These strings, these sounding strings must eternally
>   play and cry,
> The frenzied bow must eternally throb and writhe,
> Under the sun, and in the blizzard, and under the
>   whitening breakers,
> When the west is aflame, and when the east is ablaze.

The repetitions are even more insistent in the Russian than the translation indicates. All three prepositions in the third line are the same, and lines three and four begin with an emphatic repetition of the conjunction *"i"* (and).

The emphasis in Bryusov's and Ivanov's reviews on Gumilev's fantasy is perhaps somewhat misleading. While it is true that the poetry of *Pearls* still moves primarily in an imaginary world, and that the settings and personae of many of the poems are as far removed from empirical reality as in the earlier books, the tendencies noted in *Flowers* are here continued: more of the poems have their setting in the real world, and even the imagined worlds of the others are portrayed more concretely, through more precise and palpable images.

On the whole, the least successful poems of *Pearls* are the fantasy-ballads. They are the least compelling and convincing, the least viable and most dated. They smack too much of passing literary fashions and too little of the poet's individuality; they are flat in spite of their stylistic effects. "Poedinok" (The Duel) may serve as an example. The duel it describes is between the lyric I and a "maiden-warrior of ancient songs," who defeats the hero, but returns to his abandoned corpse at night to swear her love for him. The decorative surface of the style may be illustrated by the first two stanzas:

> In your coat of arms is the innocence of lilies,
> In mine are crimson flowers.
> And the battle is near, the horns have sounded,
> The shields are flashing gold.
>
> I was called out to the duel
> To the sounds of tambourines and tympani,
> Amidst the laughing paths,
> A morose Moor, like a tiger in a garden.   (I, 98)

The first two lines reveal both the poem's descent from "The Sun-Maiden" from *The Path of Conquistadors,* and its emblematic key, as does a subsequent stanza: "Terrible is the struggle between day and night, / But God has given it to us / So that people might see for themselves, / Which is destined to prevail" (I, 298).[19] The "laughing paths" and the tiger simile of the second stanza are good examples of the tendency toward superficially decorative imagery that is so characteristic of the early Gumilev, and which he only very gradually and slowly managed to overcome: images whose import is vague and which add no further dimension to the poem, which fail to fulfill the poetic metaphor's primary purpose of increasing the "density" of the poetic utterance.

Midway, as it were, between such fantasy-ballads as "The Duel," "Oderzhimyi" (The Possessed), "Kamen'" (The Stone), "Androgin" (Androgyne), etc., and the realistic lyrics of *Pearls*, is the group of what might be called exotic ballads. These include the African "Lesnoi pozhar" (Forest Fire); the "conquistador" poems "Staryi konkvistador" (The Old Conquistador), "Rytsar' s tsep'iu" (Knight with Chain), and "Kapitany" (Captains); and ballads on pseudohistorical or mythological subjects: "Tsaritsa" (The Empress), "Semiramida" (Semiramis), "Varvary" (The Barbarians), "Voin Agamemnona" (Agamemnon's Warrior), and the cycle "Vozvrashchenie Odisseia" (The Return of Odysseus). As Verkhovsky says, "In *Pearls*, the poet immediately becomes most fully himself when he touches on his favorite motifs of 'exoticism,' 'travels.'"[20] One feels that the poet is on firmer ground when he takes up such subjects than he is in the more purely fantastic sphere, that he is following his own proclivities rather than literary fashion; and the greater degree of concreteness of setting and character seem to help restrain him from excesses of superficially fanciful, decorative imagery. This is not to say that in such ballads Gumilev refrains from the decorative, rhetorical, somewhat ponderous style inherited from Bryusov, but only that lapses of taste in the handling of the style are less frequent. Two stanzas from "The Barbarians" may illustrate the point:

> Slaves presented the ivory-encrusted silver trumpet
> To the herald, on a bronze salver;
> But the northern barbarians proudly frowned,
> They recalled their rovings over snow and ice.
>
> . . . .
>
> The broad square seethed and glittered,
> And the southern sky opened out its fiery fan,
> But the morose chieftain checked his frothing horse,
> With a haughty smile he turned his troops to the north. (I, 110)

The greatest achievement in this genre in *Pearls* is no doubt the cycle "Captains," consisting of four separate lyrics. Each of the four can stand on its own and indeed, the first, "On polar and on southern seas," is no doubt the most widely known and frequently anthologized poem of Gumilev's entire production. However, Gumilev did not unite them into a cycle simply because of the common theme of seafaring: there is a certain thematic movement. The first is a paean to the courage, vigor, and resourcefulness of all seafarers of past and present: explorers, privateers, whalers. The second ("All of you, Paladins of the Green Temple," I, 143–44), although it begins with a four-stanza apostrophe to a long list of mariners, both individuals ("Goncalvez and Cook, La Pérouse and de Gama, / Dreamer and tsar, Genovese Columbus! / Hanno of Carthage, Prince Senegambus, Sinbad the Sailor and mighty Ulysses") and groups (freebooters, wandering Arabs), moves from celebration of their attributes to an evocation of the invigorating effect that the contemplation of their exploits has on the poet. It makes him feel that there are still new lands to be discovered and conquered: "And it seems that there are, as of yore, lands in this world, / Where no human has set foot . . . As if not all of the stars have been counted, / As if our world has not been fully explored!" The third poem ("As soon as the old royal fort is sighted") makes a sharp shift in tone and theme, to present a "realistic" (actually stylized, in the manner of the exotic poetry of Le Parnasse, and more evocative of the eighteenth or nineteenth century than of the early twentieth) picture of the activities of ordinary sailors in port. Finally the fourth ("But there are other realms in the world"—the thematic link with the preceding poems is underlined by the conjunction) makes another sharp shift, from semi- or pseudorealistic treatment of the theme to overt fantasy. The poem's theme is the presence on the world's sea-lanes of the inexplicable, here manifested in the image of the Flying Dutchman:

> But there are other realms in the world,
> Oppressed by a tormenting moon.
> For even supreme powers, supreme prowess,
> They are forever inaccessible.
>
> . . . .

> And there the Flying Dutchman's ship
> Scuds before a gusty wind.
>
> . . . .
>
> And if, at a limpid morning hour,
> Sailors meet it on the seas,
> An inner voice forever torments them
> With an obscure portent of grief.
>
> There are so many tales told
> About the wanton, warlike rovers of the sea,
> But the most fearsome and mysterious
> For this bold band,
>
> Is the one that tells of the region—
> Yonder, beyond the Tropic of Capricorn!—
> Where lies the frightful path
> Of the captain with the face of Cain.   (I, 146–47)

The poem obviously fits into the cycle's theme of seafaring, but the first stanza seems to imply that more is intended than a simple sailor's legend. The Flying Dutchman represents the whole sphere of the uncanny underlying the rational surface of experience.

The "Captains" cycle is in several respects highly character-istic of *Pearls* as a whole. For one thing, it unites several of the major thematic concerns of the collection: the celebration of the conquistador spirit; the exotic; Parnassian "realism"; and fantasy. Furthermore, its lyro-epic nature reflects the predomi-nant lyro-epic nature of the book as a whole, with its predom-inance of short, lyrical ballads. At the poles of this group of poems lie the "pure lyrics," on the one hand, and the longer narratives on the other. The latter category is represented by "The Return of Odysseus," also a cycle, but with a consecutive narrative thread linking the individual poems; and the narrative poems "Severnaia Radzha" (The Northern Rajah) and "Son Adama" (Adam's Dream). I will return later to the topic of Gumilev's narrative poetry, but I would mention here the place-ment of the narrative poems in the first edition of *Pearls*. "Adam's Dream" is the final piece of the section "Black Pearl," "The North-ern Rajah" closes the section "Pink Pearl," and the "Romantic

Flowers" section ends with the narrative "Neo-Romantic Fairy-Tale"; the "Grey Pearl" section opens with "The Return of Odysseus" and closes with "Captains."[21] Perhaps this reflects no more than a love of symmetry, but it seems very likely that Gumilev intended it as an indication of the significance he attached to the narrative poetry.

While the solemn, rhetorical, decorative style is clearly dominant in *Pearls,* there are exceptions. In general, the more realistic and the more personal lyrics—the two characteristics do not always coincide—and the few humorous poems tend to be written in a more straightforward, down-to-earth, sometimes even light style. As Verkhovsky writes: "sometimes, alongside the tendency toward large canvases and broad strokes, or toward monumentality, there are subtle and tender colors, soft lyric tones."[22] Verkhovsky cites "Kenguru" (The Kangaroo) as an example; others could be cited, and an even more appropriate example might be "Vecher" (Evening), a poem rather reminiscent of Zhukovsky's "Noch'" (Night)[23] in its theme, tone, mood and melodiousness:

> Still another needless day,
> Magnificent—and needless!
> Come, caressing shadow,
> And clothe my troubled soul
> In your pearl-gray robe.
>
> . . . .
>
> Silence flies down from the stars,
> The moon—your bracelet—shines,
> And to me in my sleep is given again
> The promised land—
> My long-since mourned happiness.   (I, 134)

The first stanza may be quoted in Russian to illustrate the melody:

> E*schch*e odi*n* nenu*zh*nyi de*n'*,
> Ve*l*iko*l*ep*n*yi i *nen*u*zh*nyi!
> Pridi, *l*askaiu*shch*aia te*n'*,
> I du*sh*u *sm*ut*n*uiu ode*n'*
> Svoeiu rizoiu *zh*em*ch*u*zh*noi.

The lyricism of "Evening," like Zhukovsky's, is psychologically fairly direct, but still rather abstract. A more concrete lyricism, accompanied by more concrete imagery, is found in several of the poems of *Pearls*, for example "Pokornost'" (Resignation), "Roschi pal'm i zarosli aloe" (Palm groves and aloe thickets), and "Zavodi" (Backwaters). Of these, "Backwaters" has the most down-to-earth, homely setting:

> . . . .
> The reeds stirred sleepily,
> A bat flew by,
> A fish splashed in the slough . . .
> . . . And those who have a house
> Headed home
> To their blue shutters
> To their ancient armchairs
> And their round tea table.
>
> I alone stayed outside
> To look at the sleepy backwater,
> Where it's such a delight to swim in the daytime,
> And weep in the evening
> Because I love you, Lord. (I, 127; 46)

This poem, dedicated to Annensky's wife, is somewhat reminiscent of Annensky in tone and mood. The influence of Annensky, totally absent from the first two books, can be seen in a few other poems in *Pearls*: to some extent in the ballad "Semiramis," dedicated to the memory of Annensky himself, with its decadent note of lunacy, in the literal sense ("And in somber horror from the gaze of the moon, / From the moon's tenacious nets, / I feel like casting myself down from this garden, / From a height of seven hundred cubits" [I, 108]); and especially in "Chitatel' knig" (A Reader of Books): "But in the evening . . . Oh, how terrifying / Is the shadow of night behind the bookcase, behind the icon-case, / And the pendulum, motionless like the moon / That shines over the glimmering swamp" (I, 131).

Such prosaic details as those in "Backwaters," which contrast so sharply with the decorative and exotic images that are more characteristic of Gumilev at this stage, are found in only a few poems in *Pearls*. "Starina" (Olden Times) is another example; cf. the first two stanzas:

> Here is a park with deserted groves,
> Where the sleepy ripple of the grass is so melancholy,
> Where late in the evening, the bittern
> Likes to exchange calls with the frogs.
>
> Here is a house, ancient and unpainted,
> Mist seems to roll through it,
> Its echoing halls are decorated
> With paintings of paysans. (I, 124)

Although there are no specific localizing details in the poem, it must inevitably be read as an evocation of the quiescent atmosphere of the old-fashioned Russian country estate. In this context, the use of the French word *paysans* (peasants) has an ironic resonance, as a subtle allusion to one element of that atmosphere, the Gallomania of the Russian gentry. The next stanza has the rhyme *pas'ians* / *kontredans*; i.e., patience—the solitaire game—/contredance.

This stroke of sly irony makes "Olden Times" one of the few poems in *Pearls* with an element of wit or humor. Usually the humorous element is counterbalanced by an opposing strain of melancholy, as in "Olden Times" ("And my homeless heart is tormented, / Because it is under the sole domination / Of such a tedious, gloomy, / Ungilded old-fashionedness"); or in "The Kangaroo," where the dominant melancholy tone is if anything intensified by the contrast with the ludicrous figure of the kangaroo:

> He tore off bunches of resinous needles,
> For some reason chewed on them, the silly thing,
> And hopped up to me so amusingly,
> And cried out still more amusingly.
> His caresses are so clumsy,
> But I like to caress him too,
> To make his little brown eyes
> Light up momentarily in triumph
>
> . . . .

> Why doesn't he come, the distant stranger,
> The only one I love!
>
> . . . .
>
> I want to caress someone,
> Like the kangaroo caressed me.   (I, 128)

But there are a couple of poems where the light or humorous note is uncolored by any negative emotional note: "The Maestro," with its lightly fanciful evocation of the atmosphere of a concert; and the fantasy-idyll "The Marquis de Carabasse," in which the lyrical hero enjoys the quiet pleasures of his country existence. His "servant," a fairy-tale cat (Puss-in-Boots), tries to persuade him to cast off his lassitude and take up his rightful place at the royal court, but must give up the attempt in frustration:

> My kind, my educated cat
> Represses a melancholy sigh,
> And with his fine white paw
> Angrily scratches out a flea.   (I, 117)

This is fantasy, to be sure, but how far removed from the pretensions of the fantasy of *The Path of Conquistadors*!

The thematics of *Pearls* are generally similar to those of the earlier poetry. Love and death are still among the major themes, but they are separated more than in *Flowers*. The few poems where they are linked—for example, "V biblioteke" (In the Library) and "Ia ne budu tebia proklinat'" (I shall not curse you)—are among the less successful, more derivative poems in the book. Death is less prominent as a theme, occurring usually as a secondary theme; love is more prominent, and often is given a more concrete, directly lyrical treatment than in the earlier poetry. If love was an abstraction, almost a Platonic category, in *The Path*, and in *Flowers* treated primarily in metaphorical terms, as in "The Refusal" or "The Ship," in *Pearls* it is most often treated as a concrete human emotion, presented explicitly. Compare, for example, the following eight-line poem to "The Refusal":

This has happened more than once, and will happen more
    than once,
In our muted, stubborn struggle:
As before, you have renounced me,
Tomorrow, I know, you will return, submissive.

But then, don't wonder, my hostile friend,
My enemy, possessed by a somber love,
If the moans of love become moans of pain,
If our kisses are stained with blood.   (I, 132–33)

This is certainly not the best of the love poems in *Pearls*. It
suffers from the sort of infelicity of style that so often mars
Gumilev's attempts at solemnity—for example, the sixth line (in
Russian: *Vrag moi, skhvachennyi temnoi liubov'iu*)—and as a
result of this style has an artificial, derivative ring, despite the
fact that it is very likely based on Gumilev's own experience with
Akhmatova. But it does illustrate, in comparison with the love
poetry of *Flowers*, the direction of his evolution, toward a more
personal lyricism. It should be emphasized, on the other hand,
that *Pearls* manifests only tentative, hesitant steps in this direction. For some time to come, Gumilev's poetry will continue to
be the arena for an inner struggle between the impulse to lyrical
self-expression and a self-imposed emotional restraint, an apparent fear of a too-open revelation of his emotional wounds and
spiritual conflicts, a fear which results in the tendency to conceal
his inner essence behind style.

    A new major theme in *Pearls*, one which appeared as only a
minor note in the earlier poetry, is that of adventure, including
wanderings, conquest, battle. The theme occurs in a wide variety
of contexts, from the symbolism of "Orel" (The Eagle) ("The
eagle flew ever higher, ever onward, / Across the stellar threshold,
toward the Throne of Powers . . . And he flew three days and
three nights, / And died, suffocated by his bliss. / He died, yes!
But he could not fall . . . ," I, 112–13) and the stylized fantasy
of "The Northern Rajah" (". . . to burn and to arise transformed, /
To stride across a new boundary, / In order to meet, in flame
and smoke, / The Ruler of the North, the Rajah," I, 279), or
the more original fantasy of "Puteshestvie v Kitai" (Journey to
China) ("Only in China will we drop anchor, / Even though

on the way we should meet with death!" I, 119), through the exoticism of "Captains" and "The Return of Odysseus," to the realism of "Olden Times" ("Now I would have impassable steeps, / The snows of silver peaks, / And grey and black storm-clouds / Above the hollow rumble of the avalanche!" I, 124). This theme in turn is a manifestation, in more or less explicit terms, depending on the poem, of what Verkhovsky called the "pathos of endeavor," an element that will be central to Gumilev's personal and literary profile to the very end.

CHAPTER 3

The Acmeist Period (Foreign Skies)

THE period between the appearance of *Pearls* in 1910 and
Foreign Skies in 1912 was marked by the founding of the
Poets' Guild and the beginnings of the Acmeist school. When
Foreign Skies was published in April 1912, it revealed Gumilev
as, if not yet a fully formed poet, at least no longer just a prom-
ising follower of an older master.

In this book, he essentially overcomes his heavy dependence
on Bryusov and other Symbolists and strikes out on his own
individual path. That path eventually carries him a considerable
distance from *Foreign Skies,* but henceforth the evolution is
essentially an internal one.

With forty poems totaling more than 1,200 lines, *Foreign Skies*
is smaller than *Pearls,* but considerably larger than *The Path* and
Flowers. It is divided into five sections: the first, without a heading, contains sixteen short lyrics; the second, also with no heading
but dedicated to Akhmatova (the first edition of *Flowers* and
the "Romantic Flowers" section of *Pearls* were also dedicated to
her), includes seventeen generally longer lyrics and ballads.
The third, titled "From Théophile Gautier," consists of translations of five of Gautier's lyrics; the fourth, headed *"Poemy,"*
consists of two narrative poems: "Bludnyi syn" (The Prodigal
Son) and "Otkrytie Ameriki" (The Discovery of America). The
book also included, as the fifth section, Gumilev's verse drama
Don-Zhuan v Egipte (Don Juan in Egypt), which in the Struve-
Filippov edition is not included with *Foreign Skies,* but is
printed in Volume III, together with Gumilev's other dramatic
works.

Although only two years separate the two books, the difference
between the poetry of *Foreign Skies* and that of *Pearls* is striking—much greater than that between *Flowers* and *Pearls,* or

between *Skies* and the next book, *The Quiver* (1916). There is a definite sense of a new direction, and if the line of development from *The Path of Conquistadors* to *Pearls* is essentially straight, *Skies* marks the first major turn in Gumilev's creative path. In *Pearls*, he had nearly exhausted for himself the possibilities of the Bryusovian ballad and the oratorical style associated with it, and was now ready to move beyond it. Mikhail Kuzmin, in his review of the book, spoke of its "transitional character." "Differing significantly from *Pearls*," he wrote "it leads somewhere."[1] Kuzmin paraphrases a passage from Gumilev's Don Juan play: "He will imprison you in a sweet crypt / Of beautiful words and feelings not experienced," and admits that, before the appearance of *Foreign Skies*, which "opened wide the doors to new possibilities . . . and a new atmosphere," he had been rather apprehensive that Gumilev might become entrapped in such a crypt. Here he clearly referred to the derivative and artificial nature of much of Gumilev's earlier poetry, and to the escape from that potential dead end that *Skies* represents.

Skies was published when Gumilev was most actively involved in organizing and promoting Acmeism; and it is his most Acmeistic book, the one in which his poetic practice most closely accords with the theory of Acmeism. In his Acmeist manifesto, "Acmeism and the Legacy of Symbolism,"[2] Gumilev accused Symbolism of directing its main efforts into the sphere of the unknown, of fraternizing in turn with mysticism, with theosophy, with occultism. Acmeism's attitude toward the unknowable, he says, is that "the unknowable, by the very meaning of the word, cannot be known." He does not deny the validity of the mystical experience as material for poetry, but he objects to the attempts to unravel the mystery. He does not deny the significance of theology, but objects to merging it with poetry: "To always remember the existence of the unknowable, but not affront one's thinking about it with more or less plausible conjectures—this is the principle of Acmeism. This doesn't mean that it [Acmeism—E.S.] relinquishes the right to portray the soul in those moments when it trembles as it approaches other spheres; but at those moments it should only shudder, and no more. Of course, the knowledge of God, the beautiful lady Theology, remains on her throne, but Acmeists do not desire to

either bring her down to the level of literature, nor raise literature up to her adamantine chill." Sergey Gorodetsky, in an
Acmeist manifesto published together with Gumilev's, "Some
Currents in Contemporary Russian Poetry,"[3] states the objection
to Symbolism's preoccupation with the beyond in simpler and
more pragmatic terms: "The struggle between Acmeism and
Symbolism . . . is above all a struggle for *this* world, sounding,
colored, with forms, weight, and time, for our planet Earth. Symbolism, finally, by filling the world with 'correspondences,' transformed it into a phantom whose importance is determined only
by the degree to which other worlds are visible through its
translucencies, and depreciated its great intrinsic worth. For the
Acmeists, a rose has again become beautiful in itself, by virtue
of its petals, fragrance, and color, and not of its conceivable
likeness to mystical love or something else." Both manifestos
also objected to the Symbolists' deliberately imprecise use of
words, their striving to free the word from its direct denotative
value in order to emphasize and put to symbolic use its various
possible connotations.

It would certainly be no problem to find in *Skies* individual
poems that do not agree very well with the theoretical positions
of these manifestos, but there is no doubt that the general attitude underlying the articles is reflected in the book. For one
thing, one of the most striking characteristics of *Skies,* in comparison to the earlier poetry, is the almost complete absence
of fantasy, in accord with Gorodetsky's call to return poetry
to the real world. The settings and characters are no longer
purely imaginary, invented, or loosely based on legend and
literary tradition, but "real," earthly, and often rather specific.
They are such settings as Constantinople, Rhodes, the Levant, a
circus arena, a drawing room, a society ball, a railroad station;
they are such characters as a Muslim pilgrim, Harun al-Rashid,
an animal trainer, veterans of the Turkestan campaigns, a Russian tramp, or the partners in a love relationship, who often
can be related rather directly to the poet's biography.

As the last clause implies, the greater realism of *Foreign Skies*
is linked with a frankly personal lyricism. The lyricism—not confined to the love poems—is here the wellspring of the realism.
The poet is now willing to allow his poetry to express more

directly his personal emotional experience; he no longer finds it as necessary to restrain the lyric impulse, to conceal it under the trappings of a stylized fantasy-world. The prominence of this direct personal lyricism is another characteristic setting off *Skies* from the earlier poetry. Ballads in the manner of *Romantic Flowers* and *Pearls,* most of which were in some degree fantastic, and in which, as Bryusov said, "the poet disappears behind the images he has drawn," are now absent. The majority of the poems are personal lyrics. The lyro-epic impulse that underlay the earlier Bryusovian ballads is not entirely absent, but has found new forms of expression. And the dominant style has changed accordingly: while Gumilev has by no means completely abandoned the decorative style of his earlier books, it is now far less prominent, displaced by a simpler, more straightforward style. As Kuzmin says, his poems display a "more rarefied imagery and a lighter texture, a more intimate pensiveness and a simpler lyricism. . . . And we now hear more distinctly his voice, his true voice."[4]

In making a shift away from fantasy and toward more direct lyricism and less oratorical style, Gumilev may have been in some degree deliberately shaping his poetry to correspond to a theory held *a priori,* but it would be incorrect to assume that this was the major force behind the change. It is much more likely that the changes were the result of his organic development as a poet, and that his Acmeist theory was an attempt to formulate trends that he perceived in his own poetry and that of his colleagues. Nor, in spite of the definite contrast between *Skies* and the earlier books, was the new book a radical change, a completely new departure. It was, rather, an intensification of trends already present, a selection, whether conscious or not, of one of the possibilities inherent in the earlier poetry.

Let us review, in illustration of this proposition, the development of the exotic element in Gumilev. There is a strain of exoticism running throughout his work, but it takes different forms at different periods. Generally the exotic settings found in *Romantic Flowers* (Africa, ancient Rome) differ little in essence from the purely imaginary settings. The poet is not concerned with a concrete, historically or physically accurate portrayal of the distant climes or times, but rather with the

creation of a fanciful scene and atmosphere in which his imagination need not be constrained by factual reality. The nominally
Egyptian setting of "Giena" (The Hyena), for example, is
really just as imaginary as that of "Uzhas" (Terror): "For long I
wandered along the corridors, . . . Statues cast from their
niches / Their hostile gazes at the intruder . . . I met a hyena's
head / On the slender shoulders of a girl" (I, 70–71). Although
the former does not have such a fanciful being as a girl with a
hyena's head, its hyena is hardly any more real: it emerges
from its cave at night to proclaim to the moon and the stars
its spiritual affinity with Cleopatra (I, 67–68). But alongside this
type of exotic poem, there are also in *Flowers* a couple in which
the exoticism is considerably more concrete, as, for example, in
"Zaraza" (The Plague): "A ship with the long banners of the
Prophet / Approaches Cairo . . . The captain shouts and bustles, /
You can hear his sharp, throaty voice, / Among the rigging you
can see swarthy faces / And the flash of red fezzes . . . one
vagabond has scarlet spots on his cheeks . . . together with per-
fumes and silks, / The plague is entering the city" (I, 74–75);
or in the famous "Zhiraf" (The Giraffe) (I, 76–77; 37),[5] with
its highly impressionistic but only slightly fantastic portrayal
of a giraffe.

In *Pearls*, both types of exotic poems are still present: those
in which the exoticism is merely camouflaged fantasy, as in
"Semiramis," and those in which it has a more direct relation
to reality, as in "The Forest Fire" or the first and third poems
in the cycle "The Captains." But in *Foreign Skies*, all the exotic
poems are of the latter type. Their exoticism is quite concrete,
usually rather specific in its place references, and basically realistic in treatment. A stanza from "Palomnik" (The Pilgrim) may
serve as an example:

> The dour old man won't listen, he is stubborn,
> He groans as he walks, and laughs a bitter laugh,
> His robe is tattered, but a new one,
> Lilac-colored and embroidered with gold, is in his sack;
> Under his arm—a steel-sheathed oaken staff,
> Comfortable for even his decrepit hand,
> His turban is wrapped according to Shiite precepts,
> And there are ten lire sewn into his sandals.   (I, 173)

This same poem illustrates the fact that, although Gumilev's exotic poetry has some affinity with the French Parnassians, it never quite answers to the presumed Parnassian ideal of impassivity. The poem is a narrative of the pilgrimage of a humble Moslem who believes he has been summoned by Allah himself. He is too old and feeble for such a difficult journey, and will die on the way. Up to this point, to the final stanza, the narrative has been objective, but now Gumilev's personal outlook finds expression: the pilgrim will die before reaching his goal, yes, but he will be translated into Paradise, because "he has accomplished all that it is possible for a man to accomplish—and he will see Mecca." The main narrative is of a high order of poetic merit, and Gumilev obviously expended his best efforts on it, but it is just as clear that for him the description of the journey was significant not in itself, but as the occasion for the expression of one of his most deeply held beliefs: that the ultimate rewards go to him who seeks out formidable challenges and meets them to the limit of his powers, without fear or hesitation, regardless of whether he attains his immediate goal.

Some of the other exotic poems are also ostensibly objective narratives, such as "Constantinople" or "Turkestanskie generaly" (The Turkestan Generals), but here too the poet's lyric stance is clearly perceptible below the objective surface. For example, in the latter poem the reader clearly feels the poet's admiration for the mettle of these old generals, although he does not express it directly.

A few of the exotic poems are frankly lyrical, such as "Oslepitel'noe" (a title difficult to translate; the literal meaning is "That which is dazzling"):

> When, then . . . Oh God, how pure
> And how tormenting are my dreams!
> Well, what of it; wound my heart, wound it—
> I will sink into the armchair,
> I will shade my eyes from the light,
> And will cry over the Levant.   (I, 170)

or "U kamina" (By the Fireplace):[6]

> . . . .
> I dug out an ancient temple from the sand,
> A river is called by my name,
>
> And in the land of the lakes five large tribes
> Obeyed me, honored my law.
>
> But now I am weak, as if enslaved by sleep,
> And my heart is sick, grievously sick;
>
> I have learned, I have learned, what fear is,
> Buried here in these four walls;
>
> Even the glitter of arms, even the splash of waves
> Lack the power now to break this chain.   (I, 180)

The only exotic poems that lack any personal lyrical element are the four poems of the cycle "Abissinskie pesni" (Abyssinian Songs), apparently adaptations or imitations of traditional Abyssinian poetry.

The element of fantasy is not entirely absent from the exotic poetry of *Skies*. But whereas earlier the exotic element in the fantasy poems was limited to a few names or local details, which did not really alter the essentially imaginary, unearthly nature of the settings, in *Skies* the elements of fantasy are there as a sort of spice added to a basically concrete setting. In "Oslepitel'noe," for example, the fantastic elements are present as part of the legendary heritage of the Levant, alongside its historical and physical background:

> And Baghdad reigns again,
> And Sinbad wanders again,
> And struggles with demons,
>
> . . . .
>
> You led the sailors off
> Into the caves of djinns and wolves
> Who nurture ancient wrongs,
> And across hanging bridges
> Through dark-red bushes
> To Harun al-Rashid's banquets.   (I, 169–70)

While exoticism is more prominent in *Skies* than in any of the previous books, it is still a minority of its poems that could be classed as exotic. Most of the book's lyrics either are set in ordinary contemporary surroundings (e.g., "Sovremennost'" [The Present]: "I closed the Iliad and sat by the window . . . Something shone brightly—a lantern or the moon, / And the watchman's shadow moved slowly by" [I, 163]; or "Love": "How did he dare to smell so of perfume! / To play so insolently with his rings! / How did he dare to strew flowers / Over my desk and my bed! / I left the house in a fury, / But he dogged my footsteps, / Tapping with his outlandish walking-stick / On the resounding stones of the pavement" [I, 175; 51]) or have no physical setting to speak of—their theme is worked out on an abstract, psychological level, as, for example, in "Ona" (She):

> I know a woman: silence
> And a bitter weariness of words
> Dwells in the mysterious glint
> Of her dilated pupils.
>
> Her soul responds avidly
> Only to the brazen music of verse,
> . . . .
>
> She moves with such strange smoothness,
> With silent and deliberate step,
> She couldn't be called beautiful,
> But in her lies all my happiness.
>
> When I thirst for acts of self-will,
> When I'm bold and proud—I go to her
> To learn a wise, sweet pain
> From her lassitude and fever.   (I, 165)
> . . . .

The lyrics of *Skies* are about equally divided between love poems and philosophical or meditative lyrics. Four of the love lyrics are addressed to Masha Kuzmina-Karavaeva, the rest either probably or certainly to Akhmatova. Those definitely associated with Akhmatova are: "She," "Ballade" (presented to her on their wedding day), "Ukrotitel' zverei" (The Animal-Tamer, a reply to her poem "He left me at the new moon"), "Iz logova zmieva" (From a Serpent's Lair, [I, 166–67; 49]),[7] and "Zhestokoi" (To a Cruel Woman):

"I love you, forget your dreams!"—In silence
She raised her eyes, barely trembling,
And I heard the strum of sounding lyres
And the sonorous screams of an eagle.

Sappho's eagle soared triumphantly
Over the white cliff, and the beauty
Of the luminous vineyards of Lesbos
Stopped my blasphemous lips. (I, 175)

The quotations from these two poems addressed to Akhmatova
may serve to show that the intensely oratorical, decorative style
of the earlier poetry has been muted, but not abandoned. While
the pseudomedieval external trappings of armor, imperial courts,
royal robes, precious gems, etc., have been discarded, and the
style is generally much more down-to-earth, there is still a
definite proclivity for "unusual," high-sounding words and turns
of phrase (*"Ee dusha otkryta zhadno/Lish' mednoi muzyke
stikha"* [Her soul responds avidly/Only to the brazen music of
verse]; *"krasota/Bestennykh vinogradnikov Lesbosa/ Zamknula
bogokhul'nye usta"* [the beauty/Of the luminous vineyards of
Lesbos/Stopped my blasphemous lips]). If this is true of the
love lyrics, it is even more true of the meditative lyrics. Take,
for example, the diction of "Vechnoe" (The Eternal):

Ia v koridore dnei somknutykh,
Gde dazhe nebo tiazhkii gnet,
Smotriu v veka, zhivu v minutakh,
No zhdu Subboty iz Subbot;

Kontsa trevogam i udacham,
Slepym bluzhdaniiam dushi . . .
O den', kogda ia budu zriachim
I stranno znaiushchim, speshi! (I, 161)

. . . .

I am in the corridor of sealed days,
Where even the heavens are an oppressive weight,
I look into the ages, I live in the moment,
But I await the Sabbath of Sabbaths;

The end of anxieties and of successes,
Of the blind wanderings of the soul . . .

> Oh hasten, day, when I will be sighted
> And strangely enlightened!

The meditative lyrics of *Skies* are on a variety of themes, but there is a more or less explicit element of religion present in most of them. Serious reflection on religious issues—as opposed to superficial, "literary" use of isolated religious motifs, fairly common from the beginning—first appears in *Pearls*. In *Skies*, religious themes are not only somewhat more prominent than in *Pearls*, but are treated on a deeper level. In *Pearls*, the religious poems for the most part seem to be rather detached intellectual exercises on religious themes, whereas *Skies* marks the beginnings of the poetic expression of a process that was to continue for the rest of the poet's life: his search for a firm faith and his attempt to reconcile his religious impulses with the more worldly elements of his philosophical outlook, above all to reconcile the conflict between his thirst for spiritual purity and his belief in the transcendent value of intense physical experience, including sensual passion. This conflict was expressed in his poetry as early as *The Path of Conquistadors*, but at first in quite abstract, Platonic terms. With the exception of two poems in *Pearls*, it is essentially only in *Skies* that he begins to treat the problem in terms more directly related to the Christian tradition. The two exceptions just noted—the only religious poems in *Pearls* that give the impression of engaging the poet's deeper religious sentiments—are "Potomki Kaina" (The Descendants of Cain) and "On poklialsia v strogom khrame" (He swore in an austere temple).

In *Skies*, as in those two poems from *Pearls*, the religious theme takes the form primarily of a questioning of conventional Christian beliefs, as in the argument with the Beatitudes "Otryvok" (A Fragment), or in "Dve rozy" (Two Roses):

> Before the gates of Eden
> Two roses bloomed luxuriantly,
> But the rose is the emblem of passion,
> And passion is the child of Earth.
>
> One has such a tender rosy color,
> Like a maiden whose lover has made her blush,

The other glows scarlet,
Burned by the fire of love.

Yet both are on the Threshold of Knowledge . . .
Can it be that the Most High determined thus,
And admitted the mystery of the flame of passion
To the heavenly mysteries?   (I, 156)

In "Ia veril, ia dumal" (I believed and I pondered), the mood
is one of not simply questioning, but is closer to despair:

I believed and I pondered, and the light finally dawned on me:
The Creator, once he created me, handed me over forever to fate;
I am sold! I'm no longer God's! The seller has left,
And the buyer smiles at me with obvious irony.

Like a flying mountain, Yesterday rushes along at my back,
While Tomorrow lies in wait ahead, like an abyss,
I go on . . . but sooner or later the Mountain will plunge into
     the Abyss.
I know, I know, my journey is in vain.

And if I subjugate people to my will,
And if inspiration visits me by night,
And if I have knowledge of mysteries—a poet, a wizard,
Sovereign of the universe—the more frightful will be my fall.   (I, 168)

Like the gradual concretization of the exotic element, the
purer lyricism in *Skies* is also a continuation and intensification
of trends already present earlier. As Verkhovsky wrote in connection with some of the more lyrical pieces in *Pearls*, "The
lyrical music grows and leads us to ever deeper levels, deeper—
beyond the 'beautiful clarity' of the empirical reality that gave
the original impulse, the first vibration of the string."[8] Nearly all
of the love poems in *Skies*, and some of the other lyrics as well,
possess a "lyrical music" of a harmonious simplicity and direct
emotional appeal beyond all but a few of the lyrics of *Pearls*.
This music, as Verkhovsky suggests,[9] is more than a little reminiscent of Akhmatova, and perhaps to some extent was learned
from her. Perhaps the envoi to "Ballade" will be sufficient to
illustrate this music to those readers who know Russian:

Tebe, podruga, etu pesn' otdam,
Ia veroval vsegda tvoim stopam,
Kogda vela ty, nezha i karaia,
Ty znala vse, ty znala, chto i nam
Blesnet siian'e rozovogo raia.   (I, 177)

To you, my friend, I give this song,
I believed always in your path,
When you led me, at once caressing and chastizing,
You knew all, you knew that for us, too,
The radiance of that rosy paradise would shine out.

In his book *The Poets of Russia, 1890–1930*, Renato Poggioli titles the chapter on the Acmeists "The Neo-Parnassians." While there is some justification for such a label, the Parnassian ideals of plasticity and impassivity are never more than partially fulfilled in Gumilev's poetry, although certainly more in *Foreign Skies* than elsewhere. There are a few poems in *Skies* that approach pure descriptiveness, most notably "Na more" (At Sea):

Sunset. Snakelike waves roll,
Their crests no longer angry,
But they don't run in to touch
The unconquerable shores.

And only a single breaker,
A votary of the gloom, arriving from afar,
Rushes, violent, demented,
Against the shimmering cliff

And breaks with a clamorous roar,
Throwing a shred of foam to the sky . . .
But a gay boat with a Latin sail
Floats on the turquoise sea;

And the deft, sunburned helmsman
Breathes in the waves of growing dusk
And the bracing odor of pitch
From the taut lines.   (I, 157–58)

Even this ostensibly objective piece displays a lyrical stance, or at least a lyrical mood, primarily through the choice of certain epithets: "unconquerable," "violent," "demented," "gay," "bracing."

While the dominant mood in *Skies* is lyrical, the epic or lyro-epic impulse is not entirely absent, and although there are no ballads in the manner of *Flowers* and *Pearls,* there are a few ballads in a new, "Acmeistic" manner. The closest, in its element of the legendary, to the earlier type of ballad is "Margarita," an adaptation of an incident from Goethe's *Faust,* but even here there is a great difference. In the earlier ballads, the fantastic element is presented and taken at face value, but here an ironic light is cast on it, by the suggestion that Faust, far from being the possessor of secret knowledge and of the services of Mephistopheles, is just a common seducer, even though an odor of brimstone hangs over his gifts to Margaret. In the last stanza, the poet addresses her brother Valentine: "You menacingly challenge Faust, but in vain! / He doesn't exist . . . A maiden's shame invented him; / You will encounter only a scoffing scoundrel / In a ragged red cloak . . . and you will be killed" (I, 182).

The other ballads include the quasi-Parnassian "Constantinople," and "The Pilgrim," neither of which has any fantastic element, and "Oborvanets" (The Tramp, I, 182–83; 50), unique in Gumilev's poetry so far for its homely realism. There are also the imitative ballads of the "Abyssinian Songs" cycle.

The book's two major narrative poems, "The Prodigal Son" and "The Discovery of America," will be discussed in a later chapter.

CHAPTER 4

The Mature Period (1913–1921)

I The Quiver

FOUR years passed between the publication of *Foreign Skies* and Gumilev's next collection of poems, *The Quiver*. But these were busy years in both his personal and his literary biography. There was a trip to Italy with Akhmatova in 1912, his last trip to Africa in 1913, and from August 1914, his military service. He officially launched his new school with the publication of his Acmeist manifesto in January 1913. His play *Actaeon* was published in 1913, and his complete translation of Gautier's *Emaux et Camées* appeared in 1914. During this period, he also wrote, but did not then publish, his long narrative poem *Mik*, and published poetry in several periodicals, including *Apollon*, the Acmeist journal *Giperborey*, *Russkaya mysl*, *Niva*, etc.

The Quiver is about the same size as *Foreign Skies*: Forty-eight lyric poems totaling a little over 1,200 lines, not counting two fragments from *Mik*. There is no division into sections, and no epigraph.

This is the first book in which Gumilev makes extensive use of accentual meters: fifteen of the poems, nearly a third of the book, are in *dol'nik* verse, whereas the proportion of *dol'niks* in his earlier poetry is only 5 percent. Henceforth, *dol'niks* will comprise a significant portion of his poetry, and he is recognized as one of the poets, along with Blok, Zinaida Gippius, Akhmatova, Sergey Esenin, Marina Tsvetaeva, and others, responsible for introducing the *dol'nik* and establishing it as a standard metrical form in modern Russian poetry.[1]

The Quiver marks still another turning point in Gumilev's development. *Foreign Skies* was a new departure in primarily formal, external terms. There Gumilev freed himself of direct dependence on older masters, established himself as a genuine individual talent, and proved his mastery of the craft. But on the basis of *Skies* alone we could not speak of him as anything more than an accomplished, if sometimes uneven, minor poet, the author of pleasant lyrics, sometimes very fine but generally not terribly profound, with occasional indications of a potential for something greater, as in the remarkable "The Discovery of America." *The Quiver*, however, stands on a considerably higher level of achievement, gives much more consistent evidence of a high and still-developing level of poetic sensibility and intelligence.

Several critics have pointed out the significance of *The Quiver* in Gumilev's development. M. Tumpovskaya wrote, a year and a half after the book's appearance: "Only having read 'The Quiver' can we clearly sense that up to now it was impossible to discuss Gumilev's *oeuvre*. Before this book we knew only individual samples of that work. Some of them, startling in their incomprehensible, immeasurable superiority over the whole, gave the impression of a talent that is able on occasion to outdo itself. . . . 'The Quiver' no longer gives rise to such perplexity. In its verses . . . we recognize the fruits of an integral spiritual volition, a volition that through a creative effort has succeeded in overcoming the moribund element within itself, leaving *Pearls* and *Foreign Skies* far behind."[2] Verkhovsky, writing a few years after Gumilev's death, considered *The Quiver* the beginning of the second period in the poet's development: "The second period presents us with the development of those basic facets of the artistic individuality that appeared and took shape in the first period: *The Quiver, The Pyre, The Tent,* and *Pillar of Fire* can be considered in this sense as a whole, as the basis of the artistic legacy that our poet left."[3] And Professor Struve, in his introductory article to Volume II of *The Collected Works of Gumilev,* has formulated concisely, if in rather general terms, the place of *The Quiver* in Gumilev's development: "Here, it seems to me, is the turning point in Gumilev's work: formal mastery has been achieved, the development of inner maturity and depth begins."[4]

Foreign Skies was Gumilev's most "Acmeist" collection, and if the term "Parnassian" could be applied to it with some reservations, to label *The Quiver* Parnassian would be, while not wholly inaccurate, still quite misleading. The poet has not abandoned his Parnassian (or Acmeist) concern for plasticity of imagery and logical precision of vocabulary, but he has added something to it, and it is this added element—primarily a clearer sense of an integral artistic personality underlying the stylistic surface, giving it weight and body—that gives the poems an interest and significance generally greater than the poetry of *Skies*. Furthermore, in *Skies* there was a fairly clear, if not absolute, distinction between the lyric and the descriptive strains; in *The Quiver*, there is no such distinction, but rather a harmonious synthesis of the two. A poem may find its initial impulse in the description of some external phenomenon, but that impulse is given its direction and ultimate form by the interaction between the outer phenomenon and the poet's inner being.

This synthesis is perhaps most clearly apprehensible in the Italian "cycle." The poems on Italian themes, the result of Gumilev's trip to Italy in 1912, while not published in cyclical form,[5] may still fruitfully be considered together. While each poem captures a certain essence of the given locus, they are not and are not intended to be objective descriptions. Take for example "Paduanskii Sobor" (The Cathedral at Padua):

Yes, this cathedral is both wondrous and sad,
It is: temptation, joy, and menace,
Eyes, weary with desire,
Burn in the windows of the confessionals.

The organ melody swells and recedes
And swells again, fuller and more awesome,
Like blood, surging drunkenly
Through the granite veins of gloomy churches.

I should flee from these dark vaults,
From the purple, from the languorous martyrs,
From the whiteness of their naked bodies,
Before temptation possesses my soul.

To sit on the terrace and order wine
In a solitary tavern of the old quarter.
The wall there appears quite green
From the water of a sea canal.

Quickly! One final effort!
But you weaken suddenly as you go out into the courtyard,
Catholicism has spread, like wings,
Its Gothic towers into the blue.   (I, 236–37; 71)

Verkhovsky writes of this sort of synthesis: "The path to artistic
recreation is not only via a projection [of the poet's personality—
E.S.] into the tangible objects of his world, but also a penetration
into the spiritual world of man and into the very soul of the
objects; the method of portrayal and the means of figuration—
alongside verbal painting and sculpture—is the liberation and
harmonizing of that inner musical element, which gives life and
breath both to the poet's soul and to the object portrayed."[6] After
several examples from the Italian cycle, he continues: "Thus we
at first see, as it were, a fusion of the poet's soul with the souls
of these cities, of the spiritual with physical reality, but then these
embodiments are revealed as stages in the wanderings of the soul
itself."

Much the same is true of the poems about war, which are at
once both a new theme in Gumilev, as the artistic fruit of his
combat experience, and simply a new manifestation of one of the
major constants of his poetry, the "pathos of endeavor." The war
poem with the strongest personal lyrical element is "Nastuplenie"
(The Attack):

> I cry out, and my wild voice
> Is as brass striking on brass,
> I am the bearer of a lofty idea,
> And I cannot, I cannot die.
>
> Like hammers of thunder
> Or the waters of raging seas,
> The golden heart of Russia
> Beats rhythmically in my breast.[7]   (I, 240–41)

Gumilev does not seem to be able to achieve as harmonious a
synthesis of the lyrical and descriptive elements in the war poems
as in the Italian poems. The two stanzas just quoted, in the
exuberance of their imagery and the fervor of their diction,
somewhat overwhelm the more descriptive lines. Much the same

is true of those stanzas of "Iambic Pentameters" that deal with the war. "Solntse dukha" (The Sun of the Spirit), on the other hand, which expresses the poet's personal convictions, but in more impersonal, or suprapersonal terms, is a more successful poem, more restrained and balanced.[8]

The poem "Voina" (War) provides a good illustration of the constant tension in Gumilev between his Acmeism and his penchant for the oratorical style and the weighty image that overbalances the other images, and whose presence in the poem is due more to the poet's desire to load the poem with significance— "Gumilev wants to express too much, and to fully exhaust this plenitude," as one critic has said[9]— than to an organic relationship with the other images.

> Like a dog on a heavy chain,
> A machine-gun barks beyond the forest,
> And the shrapnel buzzes, like bees,
> Collecting bright-red honey.
>
> And the "hurrah" in the distance is like the song
> Of reapers, ending a hard day's labor.
> You would think this was a peaceful village
> On a most blissful evening.
>
> And truly, it is splendid and sacred,
> This majestic business of war,
> Seraphims, bright and winged,
> Hover at the soldier's backs.
>
> Bless today, oh Lord,
> The toilers who move slowly
> Over the blood-soaked fields,
> Who sow heroic deeds and reap glory.
>
> Like the hearts of those who bend over the plow,
> Like the hearts of those who pray and grieve,
> Their hearts burn before You,
> Burn as wax candles.
>
> But grant, oh Lord, strength
> And the regal moment of victory, to him
> Who will say to his defeated foe, "Dear friend,
> Accept my fraternal kiss!"   (I, 212–13)[10]

The similes of the first stanza are excellent examples of Acmeist imagery: concrete and precise, they are chosen to present the sounds of war in terms of more common, familiar experience. The comparison of gunfire to a dog's barking is made still more vivid and appropriate by the phrase "on a heavy chain," which suggests that the dog is a large and vicious one, whose bark would all the more resemble the loud, abrupt, vicious chatter of a machine-gun, and which also suggests the metallic clank that accompanies the firing of a heavy machine-gun. In the second simile, the primary ground for comparison, the sound similarity, is supplemented by a second similarity—the ability to wound. This second meaning is then taken up and vivified by the metaphor in the fourth line (red honey = blood). The homely images of this first stanza lead into the imagery of the second stanza, which is continued in the fourth and fifth, and which is an original treatment of the traditional metaphor presenting battle as agricultural activity.[11] The word "blissful" (*blagostnyi*) in the eighth line prepares for the introduction of the religious note that dominates the rest of the poem. This religious element is on the whole well integrated with the agricultural imagery, but within this generally harmonious artistic system, discordant notes are sounded in the third and especially the last stanzas. The tone of the fourth and fifth stanzas, calling for the Lord's blessing on the humble, pious toilers in the fields of battle, is rather at variance with that of the third, with its "splendid," "sacred," and "majestic," and the somewhat disconcerting presence of seraphim; even more disconcerting is the quasi-chivalric twist that the final stanza gives the poem.

The Italian poems and the war poems comprise the chief meeting point in the collection of the descriptive and lyrical strains. Both strains also exist in purer form, and, in particular, there is a rather large group of more directly lyrical poems. The most significant of these is "Piatistopnye iamby" (Iambic Pentameters. I, 222–25). In this autobiographical poem, Gumilev casts a retrospective glance over his life, and an anticipatory gaze into his future. The poem exists in two versions. The first half, which is the same in both versions, treats his next-to-last trip to Africa, the spiritual change that he felt he underwent at that time ("And that which was formerly beyond my ken: / Disdain for the world and a weariness of dreams. / I was young, I was ardent and confident, / But the spirit of the earth was silent and haughty, / And my dazzling dreams died / As birds and flowers die. / Now my voice is slow and measured, / I know, my life has turned out badly . . ."), and his break with Akhmatova. In the first version, written in 1912, the poet has found meaning for his life, after failure of his earlier dreams, in a vaguely defined religious mission. He portrays himself as a mason, or perhaps a Mason:

> Piously raising the walls of a temple
> Pleasing to earth and to the heavens.
> Many of us are gathered here with hammers,
> And we find more joy in working together;
> A single love binds us . . .
> . . . .
> The temple rises higher, triumphant and wondrous
> . . . .
> And we, stonemasons of all times and lands,
> Hear the summoning voice of the Master.   (I, 302)

The second version, written in 1915, naturally reflects Gumilev's war experience. The religious note is still present, but in this version the poet is led to it by way of the war theme. It is as if the experience of battle—for Gumilev a religious one—pointed out to the individualist the possibility of fulfillment on a suprapersonal plane, but it is in the religious sphere that he seeks that fulfillment. Thus he finds his meaning through, but not in, war:

> And in the roar of the human throng,
> In the rumble of the passing cannon,
> In the incessant summons of the battle trumpet
> I suddenly heard the song of my fate,
> And I ran where the people were running,
> Repeating submissively: so be it, so be it.
> . . . .
> And my soul burns with happiness
> From that moment on; it is joyful,

> Serene and full of wisdom, it converses
> With the stars about God,
> Hears the voice of God in the alarms of battle,
> And deems its own paths divine.
>
> . . . .
>
> On the empty sea there is a monastery
> Of white stone, with golden domes,
> Illumined by unfading glory.
> Oh to abandon the deceitful world and go there
> To look on the expanses of water and sky . . .
> Into that gold and white monastery!

As the last stanza shows, the religious impulse has also changed its character in comparison with the first version, from active to more passive and contemplative.

"Iambic Pentameters" contains most of the major themes of the personal lyrics of *The Quiver*: love, war, exotic travels, and religion. The love theme is much less prominent in *The Quiver* than in *Foreign Skies*. Only a few poems are love lyrics, and except for the passage on Akhmatova in "Iambic Pentameters," they are rather abstract in tone. These are poems about Love, rather than poems of his love for a woman, as may be seen in "Na ostrove" (On an Island) and the two poems headed "Canzonets."

Religious motifs, on the other hand, are much more pervasive than in *Skies*. There is a clearer note of conventional Orthodox piety and faith, especially in the war poems, but there is also still a strong note of conflict between the poet's thirst for belief and his more earthly desires. The conflict is stated most directly in "Ia ne prozhil, ia protomilsia" ("I have languished, not lived"):

> I have languished, not lived
> Through half of my earthly life,
> And now, Lord, You appear to me
> In the shape of an impossible dream.
>
> I see the light on Mount Tabor
> And I feel a great remorse
> That I have so loved the land and the sea,
> The whole deep sleep of existence;

That my youthful powers
Have not submitted to Yours,
That the beauty of Your daughters
So acutely torments my heart.

But really, is love but a little red flower
That has only a moment to live,
But really, is love but a small flame
That is easily extinguished?

With this quiet, melancholy thought
I will somehow drag out this life;
But You look to the next one,
I've ruined one as it is.   (I, 245; 74)

The poem "Rai" (Paradise, I, 251–52) expresses more confidence that the conflict can be reconciled. The poet appeals to St. Peter for admission into Paradise, and calls on various saints to attest to his qualifications. St. Thomas will show that he held to church dogma; St. George will attest to his martial exploits; and "St. Anthony can confirm/That try as I might, I couldn't subdue the flesh./But then St. Cecilia's lips/Will whisper that my soul is pure." To be sure, the poem also includes the rather unorthodox argument that he should not be sent to Hell because his passions are too powerful for Hell to contain—"My love will melt the infernal ice,/And my tears will extinguish the fires of Hell"—and that therefore Lucifer also will intercede for him. To be sure, the poem is executed in only a semiserious vein, but the central belief—or hope—that an essential core of purity can be maintained despite sensual transgressions is quite a serious matter for Gumilev.

Many of the poems in *The Quiver*, while not primarily on religious themes, include religious motifs and references. This is true of all the war poems. The main theme of "Fra Beato Angelico" is art, but the content of Angelico's art introduces a strong religious element into the second half of the poem, and leads to an explicitly religious conclusion: "God exists, and the world exists, and they live forever,/While the life of man is momentary and wretched,/But he contains all within himself/Who loves the world and believes in God" (I, 218). Here again Gumilev expresses the faith that love for the earthly is consonant with belief in God.

The strong note of exoticism of *Foreign Skies* and the earlier poetry, connected primarily with Africa and the Levant, is almost absent from *The Quiver*. There is a certain exotic flavor in the Italian poems, but they are first of all descriptions of specific Italian locales, and for the most part do not deal with the lure of travel and adventure, as Gumilev's exotic poetry elsewhere tends to do. His travel poems are of course but one more manifestation of the central "pathos of endeavor," which in *The Quiver* finds its primary expression in "Iambic Pentameters" and the war poems.

We have seen above that one of the processes in Gumilev's early development was the gradually increasing concreteness of his poetry, from the wholly imaginary, highly abstract settings of *The Path*, to the ever more concrete, earthly settings of *Romantic Flowers*, *Pearls*, and *Foreign Skies*. Even as late as *Skies*, however, the concrete settings, while earthly and "real" enough, are still rather vaguely placed in space and time. The exotic poems of 1908–12, for example, are associated with North Africa and the Near East, but not many are linked with a more specific geographical location, and the few that are—Cairo ("The Plague"), "Constantinople," "Rhodes"—are chronologically vague, and could be placed anywhere within a range of at least a couple of centuries. Settings explicitly linked with contemporary reality are virtually absent throughout *Pearls*, and are infrequent in *Skies*. The process of growing concreteness and specificity of settings continues in *The Quiver*. The Italian poems are of course quite specific in their locales. The war poems lack geographical references, but, while on one level they are about the generalized phenomenon of war, they at the same time have to do with World War I, if only by virtue of such contemporary references as those to machine-guns and shrapnel.

One manifestation of the gradual confluence of Gumilev's poetic world with the world surrounding him is the appearance of the theme of Russia. Actually only three of the poems of *The Quiver* have explicitly Russian settings—"Pamiati Annenskogo" (In Memory of Annensky), "Starye usad'by" (Old Estates), and "Pochtovyi chinovnik" (The Postal Clerk)—but on the background of the generally exotic and fanciful worlds of his previous poetry, they stand out sharply. They are not, to be sure, the very first occurrences of Russian motifs in Gumilev, for the Russian theme had made a few tentative appearances, as it were, earlier. The addressee of "To a Young Girl" (*Foreign Skies*) is compared to a Turgenev heroine, and Kiev is mentioned in "From the Serpent's Lair" (*Skies*), a stylization in the manner of Russian folk poetry. The heroes of "Turkestan Generals" are old Russian generals, but the poem's emphasis is on their martial character and their exploits in the Central Asian marches of the Empire, rather than on their Russianness or the Russian milieu.

If the old-fashioned manor house of "Olden Times" (*Pearls*) is Russian only by implication, there is no ambiguity as to the setting of "Old Estates" (I, 215–16). The word "Rus" (Russia) occurs three times, and even without the geographical name, the cultural references would be sufficient, at least for anyone at all attuned to the cultural ambience of the middling Russian gentry of the late Empire. The critic Boris Eikhenbaum may have been right when he asserted in his review of *The Quiver* that "as yet Gumilev doesn't have a handle on Russia" (*Rus' poka ne daetsia Gumilevu*), that "it isn't enough to call Russia 'mysterious' and it is too extreme to call her 'a stern sorceress.' "[12] But here he reproaches Gumilev with not achieving something that he never intended to achieve. "Old Estates," in spite of its density of realistic detail ("Rickety two-story houses,/The threshing-barn, the cattle-yard/Where pompous geese converse/ Unceasingly by the trough./Roses and nasturtiums in the gardens,/ Carp in the overgrown ponds"), does not aim primarily at a physical description of the Russian country estate, but at an evocation of the oppressive weight of tradition in that milieu, including traditions of both religious and superstitious belief, as well as of social conventions. The diction that Eikhenbaum objects to may be unnecessarily vague, but in this context it is not really inappropriate. For instance, the immediate context of the epithet "mysterious" is the sentence "Old estates are scattered/Throughout mysterious Russia," which is followed by three stanzas referring to elements of superstition and religion.

The sentence "Oh Russia, stern sorceress,/You have your way in everything" occurs after a passage implying the suicide of a young girl because her father refused her permission to marry her suitor, a social unequal.

In "Pochtovyi chinovnik" (The Postal Clerk, I, 260–61) there is none of the elevated diction of "Old Estates." This is an unpretentious little ballad of domestic tragedy, a stylization in the manner of the sort of romance popular among the urban petty bourgeoisie (when first published in a magazine in 1914, it had the title "Motif for Guitar"). The first-person title character tells his own sad tale: "She's gone... The sprigs/Of blue lilac have withered,/And even the finch in his cage/Is crying over me... By now she's in Paris,/Or maybe in Berlin... And we'll never bring the runaway/Back to our quiet corner." The Russian flavor of the poem derives from the indirect cultural allusions associated with the given level of Russian society, such as the hero's position as *chinovnik*, i.e., civil servant or clerk; the finch that he keeps in a cage; the "sexton" (*psalomshchik*) in a top hat, who has suffered a similar fate and with whom he shares his grief over tea; and from the colloquial phraseology.[13] The evocation of the cultural milieu here is successful enough to give the lie to Eikhenbaum's claim that the Russian theme is out of Gumilev's province.

"The Postal Clerk" is not the only realistic personative ballad in *The Quiver*. There is "Staraia deva" (The Old Spinster), in which all the cultural references are French—plateaux, cavaliers, page, Paris, Versailles—but the atmosphere evoked is just as characteristic of the quasi-French cultural milieu of the Russian gentry as of France itself. There is also "Kitaiskaia devushka" (A Chinese Girl), which has an exotic setting but the same sort of "cultural realism" as "The Postal Clerk" and "The Old Spinster."

Besides the realistic ballads, there are two fantastic ballads in *The Quiver*, "Leonard" and "Skazka" (A Fairy Tale). Their fantasy looks forward to the fantasy of the late Gumilev, rather than back to that of the earlier Bryusovian ballads, in that it is more original, less "literary" and derivative, although based on traditional motifs. The title hero of "Leonard" saves a vaguely medieval country by a combination of arcane and military knowledge, and becomes its king. When the people ask him to

take a queen, his only answer is a sad silence, and that night
he disappears:

> Whence—no one knew.
>
> Only a shepherd boy, who was sleeping
> That night in the gloomy mountains,
> Said he had clearly heard
> A harmonious rumble of voices.
>
> As if a soaring eagle,
> A ram, a man, and a lion
> Were wailing, singing, calling,
> Speaking all at once in the darkness.　(I, 230)

"A Fairy Tale" (I, 255–57), with its light, humorous tone and
style, which almost seems to be aimed at children, has some
affinity with "Neo-Romantic Fairy-Tale" of *Romantic Flowers*.
The personae form a strange company, consisting of a devil, a
raven, a werewolf, a hyena, and a strange creature part bird and
part kitten, who is the issue of cohabitation of the werewolf and
the hyena. They are wont to howl away the night on the banks
of the river Elizabeth, and then play dominoes: "Once they
gathered together as usual,/And when they had howled excel-
lently over the river,/They sat down to their game, as always./
And they played, and played, and played,/Like they probably
had never played/Before, to the point of stupor and gasping"
(I, 256).

The fantasy of the late Gumilev is generally of two types,
which might be labeled "traditional" and "personal." The former
is based on traditional motifs of fantasy from folklore and literature, although it may involve a highly original use of these
motifs, as in "A Fairy-Tale." The latter is entirely of the poet's
own invention, and often seems to be, as it were, a transcription
or a transformation of his dreams and nightmares. The personal
fantasy is present in several poems in *The Quiver*, for example
in "The Bird," in which the poet sees a fabulous, menacing bird
with flaming eyes hovering over him:

> And I hear a smothered scream,
> Like the clang of corroded cymbals,

> Like the roar of a distant sea,
> A sea, pounding the cliff-face.
>
> And I see claws of steel
> Descending on me,
> Like tremulous swells of a river
> Illumined by the moon.   (I, 231)

He is fearful and perplexed about its significance. It can't be
Zeus's eagle, for he is no Ganymede, and if it is the Dove of
the Spirit come to summon him to Heaven, why is it so unlike
the familiar image of a dove? The poem, then, is an expression
in nightmarish imagery of a vague, uneasy sense of doom.

The atmosphere of "Razgovor" (A Conversation, I, 219–20)
is less nightmarish, but just as unreal and dreamlike, although
rather more cerebral. It resembles more a conscious meditation
cast in imaginative terms than a transcription of a dream. The
conversation is between the earth and the poet's body, which is
obliged, rather than gratifying its mundane desires, to follow
the poet's soul on her nocturnal wanderings, listening to "imaginary voices" and seeking·"nonexistent, but golden realms."
The body appeals to the earth for release from bondage to "this
fanatic" (*eta besnovataia*), but the only release the earth can
suggest is to "return to me, my child, become again muddy silt,"
i.e., suicide by drowning, a fairly frequent motif in Gumilev.

The juxtaposition in this poem of two spheres—the "nonexistent
realms" that the soul seeks, and empirical reality—recurs in many
Gumilev poems, including several others in *The Quiver*. Compare,
for example, the opening of "Na ostrove" (On the Island, I,
227–28):

> There are such heights above this island,
>   Such a mist!
> The Apocalypse was written here,
>   And here Pan died!
>
> But there are others: with palms, and meadows
>   Where the reaper is gay....[14]

On this metaphorical Patmos, the poet plays his violin, emblem
of his poetry, under "a rain of stars," while on one of the "other"

islands, he kisses and embraces a girl. He seems unable to determine which world is real. Midway in the poem it seems to him that it is only by a spell that he finds himself on Patmos, but at the end he asks himself if the ecstasy he feels with the girl is nothing more than "the moans of the violin/Under the gaze of the stars." Thus, at least, he wrote in a later variant, published in 1918; in *The Quiver*, the ending is less ambiguous: both worlds—the poet's world and the external world—exist, but "only for a moment is a bridge lowered/From your country to mine./Vast constellations: swords, crosses, and dippers/Will burn it down."

True poetry is always the product of the poetic imagination, and the line between fantasy and subjective refraction of empirical reality cannot be absolute. In Gumilev's canon, the treatment of reality is most objective, as per Acmeist theory, in *Foreign Skies*. In *The Quiver*, there are a number of descriptive poems in a more or less objective vein, but overall the subjective element is stronger than in *Skies*. In some of the Italian poems, for example, the subjectivity of the description is so strong as to introduce a definite note of fantasy, as in "Venice" ("Perhaps this is only a joke,/The sorcery of stone and water,/A mirage? The traveler is terrified:/What if it all disappears?" I, 214) or "Pisa" ("Satan, in an unbearable brillance,/Has broken free of the ancient fresco/And bends, with his age-old anguish/Over the leaning tower of Pisa," I, 226). In such images, and particularly the latter one, the poet's subjective anxieties become so powerful that they are suddenly projected outward, and become a palpable element in the physical scene being described. As Tumpovskaya writes: "Thus, not content with even the most vivid and heroic element that he can discover in real, earthly life, he extends its limits and brings his poetry into the world of fantasy. This transition takes place automatically, barely noticeably; in Gumilev's poetry, fantasy itself is only a perceptible extension of reality." And again: "His senses lose all limit and measure, they outgrow themselves, separate from their bearer, become waking visions . . . hallucination achieves real existence. . . ."[15]

There are also descriptive poems in which there is no explicit element of fantasy or unreality, but where the subjective refrac-

tion of the physical scene results in a dreamlike, semireal atmosphere. Such is "Vecher" (Evening, I, 249; 73): "On such tedious
evenings/Coachmen drive their horses headlong,/Fishermen
rend the water with their oars,/Woodcutters hack savagely/
At huge bushy oaks . . .": *V takie medlennye vechera/Konei*

kar'erom goniat kuchera,/Sil'néi veslóm rvút vódu rybakí,/

Ozhestochénnei rúbiat lesnikí/Ogromnye, kudriavye duby. . . ."
These lines quoted in Russian illustrate Gumilev's technical skill:
the conglomeration of gutterals and the rolling Russian "r," the
jerky rhythm, especially in the third and fourth lines, and the
violence of the verbs all contribute to the creation of an atmosphere consonant with the theme of man's desperate efforts to
overcome the ponderously inert resistance of nature.

The poem "Dozhd'" (Rain) shows a similar subjectivity of
description:

> Through window-panes spattered with rain,
>   The world seems blotched to me.
> But as I look, nothing in it has faded,
>   Nothing has become alien.
>
> Only the greenery has become a bit more ominous,
>   Like a splash of vitriol,
> But thanks to this, the round bush of blood-red roses
>   Stands out more sharply.
>
> The splashing of drops in puddles is more deliberate now
>   And they murmur their psalm
> Like nuns at the evening hour,
>   In a rapid little voice.
>
> Glory, glory to the black-clouded sky!
>   It's like a river in springtime, where
> Instead of fish, the trunks of mountain trees
>   Toss in the turbid waters.
>
> In the foul sloughs of enchanted millponds
>   Is heard the neighing of frenzied horses,
> And the soul, that most hapless of captives,
>   Finds relief and respite here.   (I, 248)

Gumilev never aimed at complete objectivity in his verse, even in *Skies,* but a comparison of "Rain" with a poem like "At Sea" will show how much stronger the subjective element is in *The Quiver* than it was in *Skies.* As the process of inner growth that Professor Struve refers to began, Gumilev was growing beyond not only the conventional, derived, and contrived worlds of his early poetry, but also beyond the limiting confines of his "neo-Parnassianism."

II   The Tent

The first edition of *The Tent* was published in 1921, in Sevastopol,[16] but the poems were written earlier. There is some question as to how much earlier. The first edition carried the subtitle "Verses of 1918," but in the volume of selected poetry of Gumilev published by his younger colleague Nikolay Otsup in 1959,[17] the editor dates the selections from *The Tent* to 1907–13, giving these dates in parentheses on the title page of that section, which Otsup placed between selections from *Foreign Skies* and those from *The Quiver.* This is presumably one of the sources referred to in the commentary to *The Tent* in the Struve-Filippov edition: "The first edition appeared . . . with the subtitle 'Verses of 1918,' which refutes the opinion sometimes expressed that Gumilev wrote these poems much earlier" (II, 296). A refutation equally as strong as Gumilev's dating is the poems themselves: they most certainly were not written, at least in their published form, between 1907 and 1913. There is a vast difference in tone, style, and texture between them and the poetry of *Romantic Flowers* and *Pearls,* and a lesser but still notable difference from that of *Foreign Skies.* Otsup's dating might be based only on the assumption that they were written during Gumilev's trips to Africa, or there may have been a stronger basis, namely, the poet may have kept notes for African poems during his trips there, which he worked up into completed poems only in 1918. This theory would also help explain the vividness of many of the descriptive passages, which seems quite unusual for memories five to ten years old. In any case, none of the poems in either edition of *The Tent* appeared in print before 1921, as far as we now know.

Chronologically, then, the poetry of *The Tent* would seem to come after that of *The Pyre* (written between 1915 and 1917), but I have chosen to discuss it here in order to avoid an interruption between the sections on *The Pyre* and *The Pillar of Fire*, which are closely linked by certain lines of development.

The Tent is a very specialized book, a collection of sixteen lyrics all devoted to Africa, "a unique phenomenon in Russian letters."[18] Most of them are quite long: all but two are over forty lines, and two are over a hundred lines. The book is not only monothematic, but virtually monometric: fourteen of the poems are in anapests, and the other two are in anapest-based *dol'niks*, i.e. *dol'niks* with a regular two-syllable anacrusis.

After the opening poem, entitled "Vstuplenie" (Prelude), an invocation of the whole continent ("Hanging like a gigantic pear/ On the ancient tree of Eurasia"), the book divides into two nearly equal parts. The first includes eight poems devoted to countries and regions of Africa that Gumilev had seen in person (Egypt, the Sudan, Abyssinia and Somaliland, the Suez Canal and the Red Sea), followed by seven devoted to places he hadn't seen, but had obviously read and heard about extensively; that is, West Africa, including Liberia, Dahomey, the Niger River; and Central and South Africa, with the equatorial forest, Damara, the Zambezi River, and Madagascar.

There is no formal or typographical indication of a division into sections, but there is a clearly perceptible difference between the two parts. The poems of the first part are generally much more concretely and realistically descriptive, while in those of the second part the descriptive element is less prominent, and the descriptions have a rather more abstract air, reflecting the fact that they are given at second-hand. Notes of fantasy, while present in both parts, are stronger in the second. The second part has three of the book's four balladlike poems, and its only humorous piece ("Liberia," a rather tasteless mockery of the attempt to transplant a European-style republic and civilization into black Africa).

The notes of fantasy in the second part are of two types. In one type, the fantasy is at least ostensibly based on tribal folklore, as in "Zambezi" and "Damara." The latter (II, 100–101), subtitled "Hottentot cosmogony," gives Gumilev's version of the

Hottentots' conception of their origin—and that of the related tribe of Bushmen—from a fabulous gigantic bird that was torn into two parts when it attempted to challenge God. From the upper, singing part arose the Hottentots, who "sing and sing, without care"; the Bushmen were born of the lower part. "Zambezi" (II, 97–99; 61) is a ballad in the form of a song sung by a Zulu warrior, to whom "the spirits of the fog" appeared to foretell to him his career as a fearsome and fearless warrior, a "worthy descendant of Dingan,/A destroyer, killer and lion," and his death on the tusks of a rogue elephant. "Dahomey," another ballad, has the air of a retelling of a tribal legend, describing how a ruler pronounced the death sentence—possibly part of a religious sacrifice—on one of his generals. The third ballad in this second part of the book, "Ekvatorial'nyi les" (The Equatorial Forest), has more of the ring of popular adventure tales of European origin than of either tribal tradition or personal experience. The poet encounters a French explorer, lost in the jungle, wounded and wracked by fever, and listens through the night to his delirious ravings about how he was captured by and escaped from cannibalistic pygmies. This poem contrasts with the one ballad in the first part, "The Somali Peninsula" (II, 91–93; 62–63),[19] a first-person narrative of preparations on the eve of a battle with Somali tribesmen. The incident related here may be partly or largely invented, but it has a much more authentic ring to it than the narrative of "The Equatorial Forest."

The other type of fantasy in the second part is personal rather than legendary in nature. It springs from the poet's own imagination and psyche. Let us take as an example the dream-setting of "Madagascar":

> My heart pounded, mortally sad,
> All day long I wandered, anguished,
> And that night I dreamed I was sailing
> Down some great river.
>
> The river was wider and wider
> And brighter and brighter with each moment,
> I was in a completely unknown world,
> And my boat was so light.

> A red idol on a white stone
> Told me the secret of the spell,
> A red idol on a white stone
> Cried out loud, "Madagascar!"
>
> . . . .
>
> And I sighed: Why am I sailing,
> Why don't I remain here?
> Isn't it here, after all, that I'll sing
> My best poems?
>
> But my voice couldn't be heard,
> And no one could help me,
> And the warm night descended
> On the wings of a bat.
>
> The sky and the forest darkened,
> The swans fell silent in forgetfulness . . .
> . . . I was lying on my bed,
> Mourning for my boat.   (II, 96–97)

The dream motif recurs in the last stanza of the book's last poem, "Niger":

> The heart of Africa is full of song and flame,
> And I know that, if we have at times
> Dreams for which we can find no name,
> They come to us, Africa, on your winds!   (II, 106)

This poem brings the collection to a harmonious close, with its echo of the first stanza of the introductory poem:

> You are deafened by howls and the clatter of hooves,
> You are enveloped in flame and in smoke,
> My Africa, and the seraphs of heaven
> Speak about you in a whisper.   (II, 71; 57)[20]

"Prelude" sets the tone for the whole book, with its religious motifs (the seraphs of the first stanza think with implied concern about the "inexperienced" guardian angel assigned to Africa; her history is referred to as her Gospel; Christ and the Virgin are mentioned in the last line), and its combination of elements of fantasy with realistic detail:

> Listen to the tale of your deeds
> And your fantasies, of your feral soul,
> You, who hang like a gigantic pear
> On the ancient tree of Eurasia.
>
> My destiny linked with yours, I will tell
> Of chieftains in leopard-skin cloaks
> Who lead legions of somber warriors
> To victory in the gloom of the forests;
>
> Of villages with ancient idols,
> Who smile an evil smile,
> And of lions who stand over the villages
> And switch their ribs with their tails.

The element of fantasy is stronger in the second part, and the realistic element more dominant in the first part, but these are only tendencies, and the two elements are interwoven throughout. Although there are occasional references to native lore in the first part (e.g., "Here a wizard performs his customary miracle," II, 88), the fantasy in this part stems mainly from the poet's own imagination, as in the scene of the future that he imagines at the end of "The Sahara," when that desert will have overflowed its boundaries to cover the Mediterranean Sea, Paris, Moscow, and Athens, "And when, at last, Martian ships/ Appear at our earthly globe,/They will see an unbroken golden ocean/And will give it the name of Sahara" (II, 81).

But far more pervasive, and more determinative of the overall effect of the collection than the explicit elements of fantasy, is the generally fanciful atmosphere that Gumilev creates in his images of Africa. It is as if for the poet Africa were at once a real, physical region of Earth, and a land of the imagination, where even the most solid and real elements of the landscape are permeated with a fantastic essence, which stems partly from the highly exotic aspect of African nature and human culture, and partly from the poet's projection of his own attitude into the empirical reality of the continent. The interpenetration of the poet's psyche and external reality that we observed in the Italian cycle of *The Quiver* is here continued and intensified, and in this respect *The Tent* assumes its proper place in the line of Gumilev's development as another link between the realism of *Foreign Skies* and the amalgam of realism and fantasy that we find in *The Pyre* and *Pillar of Fire*. As Verkhovsky writes in connection with *The Tent*: "This is one of the paths of that genuine realism, toward which the poet is moving, in this case—the realism of the fantastic (*realizm skazochnogo*): realistic fantasy, the only genuine fantasy, has a primal significance in his development."[21] This aspect of the poetry of *The Tent* is so pervasive that illustrative passages could be quoted from nearly every poem in the book. No matter how accurate and concretely evocative any given descriptive passage may be, it is almost invariably either surrounded by or intertwined with elements of the fanciful. These elements sometimes derive from the objectively "fantastic" nature of the scene itself, as in the following passages: "Everywhere there are towers, palaces of porphyry,/ All around are fountains and palm trees on guard—/This is the sun, painting with the radiant brush of mirage/On the smooth surface of aerial mirrors" ("The Sahara," II, 78–81); "And then, smiling like a little boy/Who has thought up an amusing joke,/ He ["God's gardener"—E.S.] collected here quite fantastic,/Marvelous birds and animals" ("The Sudan," II, 83–86; the passage continues with descriptions of parrots, elephants, lions, leopards, rhinoceroses, and gazelles); "Everything that I drew near to here,/Was larger than anything I had seen before:/I watched giantesses tending huge camels/By broad ponds./I watched as towering Galla tribesmen,/In leopard and lion skins,/Cut down racing ostriches with one blow,/At full gallop on their giant, fiery steeds" ("Gallaland," II, 90–91). Already in this last passage, there is an indeterminate point at which accurate, objective description of the exotic passes over into subjectively fanciful characterization, and such transitions are found everywhere in *The Tent*. The following example is from a description of a sandstorm in "The Sahara":

> And, like the age-old trunks of monstrous palms,
> Columns of dust rise up and swell,
> Bending and swaying, they pass through the gloom,
> And you secretly believe they will never fall.
>
> They'll go on roaming till the end of time,
> More menacing with every hour,

> Their heads disappearing among the clouds,
> These frightful grey serpents.
> . . . .
>
> And when they all settle, like new mountains,
> On the plain's smooth surface, clear now,
> The khamsin blows out to the Mediterranean
> To sow dissension and intoxication.   (II, 79–80)

The fanciful element here stems to a great degree from the poet's own imagination, but it does not draw the reader beyond the physical scene into the poet's psyche, as do many, more subjective, passages in *The Tent*. The following passage from "Egypt," for instance, introduces the motif of previous or multiple existences, which recurs several times in Gumilev:[22]

> There, gazing at the deserted waters,
> You will cry out, "But this is a dream!
> I am not chained to our age
> If I can see through the abyss of time.
>
> Wasn't I there when naked slaves,
> Carrying out the royal commands,
> Hauled stones across the deserts
> And erected these very columns?
>
> And wasn't I there, centuries later,
> When priestesses, dancing in a ring,
> Sang praises to the crocodile
> And bowed down to Ibis?"   (II, 75)

Even more subjective is the fantastic moon-motif that is interwoven with the realistic description of preparations for battle in "The Somali Peninsula":

> I remember the night and the sandy land,
> And the moon, so low in the sky.
>
> And I remember that I couldn't take my eyes
> From its golden path.
>
> It's bright there, and doubtless birds are singing
> And flowers bloom beside ponds,

> There you can't hear ferocious lions roaming,
> And filling the rifts with their roars
> . . . .
>
> And I thought, painfully, that there, on the moon,
> The enemy could not creep up on me.
> . . . .
>
> And when, at dawn, the moon was setting,
> Not the same now, but red and terrible,
>
> I understood that, like a knightly shield,
> It burns with eternal glory for heroes,
>
> And I gave the orders for placement of the camels,
> And entrusted my free soul to my rifle.   (II, 91–93)

The "pathos of endeavor," which implicitly underlies so much of the poetry of *The Tent*, is expressed explicitly here, in the form of the theme of heroism.

Alongside the elements of fantasy and fanciful description, and the elevated, oratorical style in which they are generally cast, there are occasional notes in *The Tent* of a more straightforward, down-to-earth, human affection for Africa, with even a touch of humor. Aside from the rather questionable humor of "Liberia," there is, for instance, the gently ironic portrayal of the poet's reception by the "portly Negro" ruler of Gallaland: "I bowed, and he smiled in answer/And clapped my shoulder affectionately./I presented him with my Belgian pistol/And a portrait of my sovereign./He kept asking whether they know much about him/In distant, uncivilized Russia . . ." II, 91; or the ingenuous conclusion of "Egypt":

> If a pensive stork should settle
> Nearby on your fields,
> Write a note in English
> And tie it under his wing.
>
> And in the spring, on a eucalyptus leaf,
> If the stork returns,
> You'll receive a greeting from Egypt,
> From happy fellahin children.   (II, 78)

A similar affection for Africa, though in a more serious tone, is expressed at the end of "The Sudan": "It's evening . . . It's quiet in the Sudan,/And I believe, I believe, God is bending/ Over this huge child's bed" (II, 86).

All these variations in style, tone, and theme, then, together with the great variety of natural and human scene, make of *The Tent* a denser and more multiform body of poetry than might be expected of a collection devoted entirely to one major topic, a body of poetry quite on a level with Gumilev's other late collections, *The Pyre* and *Pillar of Fire*. It is, as has been said of it, a book of "rich and picturesque variety,"[23] one in which "a powerful image arises before us—Africa itself,"[24] and which "expresses Africa as genuinely and as beautifully"[25] as any in the world's poetry.

III   The Pyre

Of the two and a half years separating the publication of *The Quiver* from *The Pyre—The Quiver* appeared in January 1916, *The Pyre* sometime after Gumilev's return to Russia in May 1918—Gumilev spent exactly a year abroad. Probably this absence from Russia, as well as the dislocations of war and revolution, explain the fact that only five of the poems in the book had been published previously in periodicals, and four of those in 1916, whereas most of the poems of *The Quiver* had been published previous to the appearance of the book.

The Pyre is the smallest of Gumilev's collections of original poetry, and the only one that did not include any long narrative pieces along with the lyrics. It consists of twenty-nine mostly short lyrics, totaling nearly 650 lines. As in *The Quiver,* almost a third of the poems are in *dol'niks.*

After a book in which the theme of love was relegated to a definitely secondary position by the themes of war and foreign travel, *The Pyre* returns the love theme to a prominence at least equal to that which it held in *Foreign Skies*. While *Skies* has, proportionately, more love poems than *The Pyre,* the theme is more diffuse in the earlier book. The love poems of *Skies,* for the most part, fall into two groups of clearly differing character:

the poems inspired by Gumilev's feeling for Masha Kuzmina-Karavaeva are less intense and more conventional than those associated with Akhmatova. Also—an extrinsic factor, but one which nonetheless affects the overall impact of the given theme on the reader—the love poems are dispersed throughout the book, intermixed with poems on other themes. The love poems of *The Pyre* are all grouped together at the end, and Gumilev had his reasons for doing this, as they are all the poetic fruit of one passion, his unrequited Paris love for Elena D. And this single inspiration is reflected in the style. In spite of definite differences in mood from poem to poem, and considerable variety in specific subjects, the poems display a clearly perceptible unity of tone: a combination of exaltation with intense but calm and resigned melancholy.

The love poems in *The Pyre* are only a part of the poetry inspired by Elena D.: while in Paris, Gumilev kept an album of the poems dedicated to his love for her, from which he chose eleven for inclusion in *The Pyre*. After his death, in 1923, the whole cycle was published in a volume entitled *To the Blue Star*, whose title derives from a line in one of the poems. The book included twenty-three poems besides those already published in *The Pyre*. The cycle should be considered as a whole, for there is nothing intrinsic to set off those included in *The Pyre* from the rest.

One very striking feature of the cycle is the fact that in spite of the single, concrete addressee, the poems are quite abstract. Whatever the actual nature of Gumilev's feeling for the girl may have been, the poems are less a record of the peripeteia of the affair than they are a revelation of a significant psychological trait of the poet: his commitment to the Romantic idea of love, his apparently continual state of being in love, not so much with a flesh-and-blood woman, as with Love itself and the Ideal Woman.

Such phrases of physical description as do occur provide an image of rather conventional beauty (a "porcelain" body, "satin" skin, etc.). By far the most insistently evoked physical feature are the eyes, but we are not even told their color (nor that of the "thick strand" of hair): they are "large," "gazellelike," "radiant," "bold," "speaking," and "singing." The epithets applied to her mouth are presumably more specific to this particular woman, but still are more subjective than precise: he speaks of her "childish mouth" and her "semi-childish lips." Even the poem entitled "Portret" (Portrait, II, 150; 135) is generalized and unspecific, as "Her porcelain body torments me/With its mat whiteness,/Like a petal of white lilac/Under the dying moon."

The phrases of physical description are far outweighed—not so much quantitatively as qualitatively—by phrases of metaphorical evocation of the impression that the beloved makes on the poet, the aura that his passion surrounds her with: "And she is all buoyant, like a bird,/In bright autumntime,/Already about to take leave/Of the sad northern clime" (II, 150); "You were my folly,/Or my wondrous wisdom" (II, 165); "Yes, in my troubled destiny,/You are a pilgrim's Jerusalem" (II, 22). Alate images, and images of fire and light, are prominent here: "Your soul is wondrously winged" (II, 154); "Your silver wings" (II, 160); "Your winged, instinctive,/Impetuous ardor" (II, 25); "In man's dark destiny,/You are a winged summons to the heights" (II, 28); "You, who are created of fire" (II, 161); ". . . You . . . appear to me/As the Lord's blinding lightning,/And henceforth I burn in a flame,/That rises from the nether world to heaven" (II, 146–47); "You entered my dark heart/Like a sunlit cloud of paradise" (II, 154); "You are but a blue star" (II, 155); "You appeared as a blinding star" (II, 164).

It is obvious from such images that the intent of the cycle is not to evoke the image of the woman as a person, but to transform her into a symbol of the significance that the experience of love has for the poet. Insofar as the cycle is autobiographical, it is concerned less with the object of his love than with registering the quality and texture of his emotional pain. Even more, however, it is concerned with establishing the role of love as a link with the Ideal.

For Gumilev, love functions in concert with poetry as an avenue to the world of the Ideal, and several poems and passages from the cycle treat the poetic inspiration that his love brings to him, as in the line, "And my verses? It is you who whispers them to me" (II, 165), or in the cosmic images of "Usta solntsa" (The Sun's Lips, II, 163; 79):

Oh no, your childish mouth and bold maiden's gaze
Can never be expunged from my destiny;
That's why, when I dream of you,
I speak and think in rhythm.

I feel the ebb and flow of vast seas
Under the pull of the moon,
And throngs of stars that move as they burn
In a motion foreordained from the beginning of time.

Oh, if you were with me always,
A smiling benison, a genuine presence,
Then I could set foot on the stars
And would kiss the sun's blazing lips.

The link between love, poetic creation, and the world of the ideal is expressed most clearly in "Tak dolgo serdtse borolos'" (My Heart Struggled So Long, II, 157–58): "I thought my voice was gone,/My ringing voice, forever./But you restored it to me . . . And returned to my memory/The radiance of white lilies and of blue worlds." The "white lily" and the "blue world" are both frequent images in Gumilev for the sphere of the ideal.

"Memory" is a key word here, with its implication that a poet's visionary insights are a form of memory, memory from his former or parallel existence (or that of his soul) in the world of the ideal. In "Canzonet 3" (II, 24; 87), which was included in *The Pyre* (a significantly different version was published in *To the Blue Star*, under the title "Obeshchan'e" [The Promise, II, 161]), love, poetry, and the ideal are similarly linked, although from a rather different viewpoint. The poet stands, as it were, in expectation of the imminent final transfiguration of earthly reality—a favored theme in Symbolist poetry—when the two levels of existence will be restored to their original unity and the poet will return to his true role of spiritual leader. Then, he says, "I will cry,/'Where are you, who is created of fire?' . . . I, the servitor of your beauty,/Will share with you my power,/Because you are the complete,/The final happiness!"

The poem that gave the title to the posthumous publication of the cycle, "The Blue Star" (II, 154–55; 78), expresses most clearly the idea of love leading to a momentary translation onto another level of existence:

I was torn out of this narrow life,
This meager, ordinary life,
By your tormenting, wondrous,
Irresistible beauty.

And I died . . . and I saw a flame,
One that had never been seen before,
Before my dazzled eyes
Shone a blue star.

Transforming my spirit and my body,
A musical strain rose, and fell again;
It was the speaking and the ringing
Of your blood, singing like a lute.

And there was a fragrance, sweeter and more fiery
Than anything found in life,
And even than that lily that grows
In the angels' lofty garden.

And suddenly, out of the radiant abyss
The earthly sphere arose again;
You suddenly appeared before me,
Trembling like a wounded bird.

You repeated, "I am suffering,"
But what can I do, knowing
At last with such sweet certainty
That you are but a blue star.

It is an essential feature of Gumilev's treatment of this theme that the transcendent experience of Ideal Love is not isolated from earthly experience. The poet returns from that other sphere to everyday life, and returns changed, with the indelible mark of that world. This idea is adumbrated in "The Blue Star," and recurs in other poems of the cycle, most clearly in one of those included in *The Pyre*, "Canzonet 1" (II, 22; 85): "Only love remains to me, calling/With a string from an angelic harp,/ Piercing my soul with the blue rays of paradise,/As if with a fine needle./You alone remain to me. In person/I have seen the sun of night,/And it is only for you that I live on this earth,/ And carry out earthly affairs."

The theme of a link between the earthly and the ideal, the

possibility of their unification or of a translation from the former
to the latter, occurs throughout Gumilev's poetry, but gains increasing prominence in his late work. In the period of *The Pyre*,
it appears not only in the love poems, but in other contexts as
well. In "Priroda" (Nature, II, 9; 88)[26] it is cast in a vein reminiscent of the nineteenth-century poet Fedor Tyutchev's view
of the physical world as a veil cast over the true reality.
In the first two stanzas, the poet evokes several elements of
nature "which the spirit does not acknowledge," then concludes:

> I see shadows and outlines,
> Seized with wrath, I see
> Only the barren variety
> Of seeds spilled by the Creator.
>
> Why try to fool me, Earth:
> Throw off your beggar's garments
> And become what you are—a star
> Shot through with flame!

In a somewhat similar poem on the illusory nature of earthly
"reality," "Prapamiat'" (Primal Memory, II, 21; 96),[27] Gumilev
uses the conventional image of life as a dream in which the
dreamer experiences vague intimations ("memories") of his
waking life, the true reality:

> And this is the whole of life! Spinning, singing,
> Seas, deserts, cities,
> The glimmering reflection
> Of that which is forever lost.
>
> A fire rages, trumpets trump,
> And chestnut horses fly,
> Then provocative lips
> Speak and speak again, it seems, of happiness.
>
> And here again are ecstasy and grief,
> Again, as before, as always,
> The sea waves its grey mane,
> And deserts and cities rise up.

> When, then, at last, aroused
> From my dream, will I be myself again—
> A simple Hindu, dozing
> By a stream in the sacred twilight?

Of particular interest in this poem are the surrealistic touches in the second stanza—a foretaste of such openly surrealistic poems in Gumilev's next book as "The Streetcar Gone Astray" and "Among the Gypsies."

The motifs of dream and another existence are also combined in "Stockholm" (II, 18–19; 90):

> Why did I have that confused, disordered dream,
> Born of the depths of other times,
> That dream of Stockholm, so disturbing,
>
> . . . .
>
> "Oh, Lord," I cried in alarm, "what if
> This land is truly my homeland?
> Did I not love here and did I not die here,
> In this green and sunny land?"
>
> And I understood, that I was lost for aye,
> In the blind passages of space and time,
> While somewhere native rivers flow,
> And the way to them is forever closed to me.

A companion piece, "Norvezhskie gory" (The Mountains of Norway, II, 16), does not involve the motifs of dream or shifting of time planes, but its atmosphere is even more nightmarish: "And wondrous are these unearthly faces,/Whose locks are snow, whose eyes are holes into Hell,/From whose cheeks, harrowed by storms, flows/Like a grey beard, a waterfall." If in "Primal Memory" and "Stockholm" the irreal world of the poem is clearly delineated as belonging to the world of dream or imagination, in "The Mountains of Norway," as in some of the poems in *The Quiver* discussed above, the line between reality and fantasy is not clearly drawn. The poet's subjective, impressionistic re-creation of the physical scene hovers on the brink of the fantastic. The objective and the subjective interpenetrate, and we can no longer determine whether such a passage represents the impact of the striking physical phenomenon on the poet's imagination, or the poet's projection of his subjective vision onto the object. For example, are the "holes into Hell" simply an effective image for the caverns, or does he sense a malevolent presence in them?

This poem provides a good example of the difference between what I have called "traditional" and "personal" fantasy in Gumilev. It contains, as it were, two crescendos of dread: the last stanza, quoted above, and the second: "Here, with screams of monstrous derision,/Like Satan on a fiery horse,/Peer Gynt flew on a frenzied reindeer/Along the most forbidding steeps." The diction here is considerably more forceful than in the last stanza, yet this stanza taken alone is less unsettling in its effect than the final stanza taken alone, because the nightmarishness is safely exteriorized, transferred to the product of another poet's imagination. In the last stanza, the reader realizes that the poet is expressing his own alarm, not merely reproducing another's vision. Actually, of course, neither stanza has its full effect in isolation; they reinforce each other.

There are several other poems in *The Pyre* with elements of the fantastic. "Zmei" (The Serpent, II, 11–12) remains entirely in the sphere of traditional fantasy; it draws on motifs from the Russian oral epics (*byliny*) and comprises a stylized ballad about an Asiatic dragon abducting Russian maidens. The rest are in the sphere of "nightmare" fantasy. "Tvorchestvo" (Creation, II, 19), for example, presents the poet's creative torments as a nightmare or vision: "Engendered by my word,/Giants drank wine/Through the night, and it was crimson,/And it was dreadful."[28] Here the nightmare vision stems entirely from the poet's mind, while in "Ledokhod" (The River Ice Breaks Up, II, 8–9; 93), as in "The Mountains of Norway," it has an external stimulus, the spectacle of the ice breaking up on the Neva River, a scene which, thanks to Gumilev's method of projection of the subjective onto the external world, becomes preternaturally ominous:

> Ice-floes pile one on another,
> Green, like verdigris,
> With a terrible snake-like hiss.

> Such shapes as weigh on geographers
> In their uneasy dreams—
> The tortuous outlines
> Of unknown continents.
>
> With an uncertain, feeble odor
> Of mushroom dankness,
> Like those secret cellars,
> Where a corpse is buried and toads roam.
>
> The river is ill, the river is in delirium, . . .

This poem illustrates how far afield Gumilev's nightmarish associations can lead—from the shifting, rustling ice-floes to toads and a concealed corpse—without the external stimulus being lost sight of.

The famous poem "Muzhik" (II, 12–14; 98–99)[29] is also built on nightmarish associations stemming from an external stimulus, but here the process is somewhat different, resulting in a very different sort of poem. In poems like "The River Ice Breaks Up," the vision is purely personal, but in "Muzhik," it is at once personal and suprapersonal. In this poem, Gumilev is concerned with the historical destiny of Russia, and moves, whether consciously or not, toward the expression of a communal dread. The poem relates how a malign peasant (clearly Rasputin or modeled on Rasputin, though his name is not mentioned) comes out of the mysterious forest depths of Russia to the capital to bewitch the Empress, and how the city rises up in alarm to exorcise this interloper. But the poem has a far greater resonance than simply that of a ballad relating *"l'affaire Rasputin,"* for Gumilev treats his muzhik as a type, as only one of many, as a representative of the dark, poorly understood forces of rural and forest Russia, where the European civilization of the capital has not penetrated and where ancient and pagan traditions still hold sway. And it is in the passages that portray the muzhik's dark origins that the nightmarish atmosphere of the poem is most intense:

> In thickets, in huge swamps,
> By a river the color of tin,
> In dark, shaggy log huts,
> There are strange muzhiks.

One such goes out into the trackless wastes,
Where the feather-grass grows wild,
And listens to the cries of Stribog,[30]
Sensing an ancient tale.

With a heavy stare
The Pecheneg used to pass through here . . .
It smells of dankness and reptiles
Alongside receding rivers.

Here he is now, with his satchel,
Filling the forest path
With a song that is lingering, soft,
But wickedly, wickedly sly.

This path is light and gloom,
A bandit's whistle in the fields,
Wrangles, bloody brawls
In dream-dreadful taverns.

The atmosphere of dread results not only from the diction and imagery of this passage, but as well from the treatment of Rasputin as not just an exceptional case, but as a representative of pagan, Asiatic, forest Russia, rising to avenge the attempt to impose on it an alien civilization. And if the threat is collective, so is the response: it is not just a court clique (as it was in reality) that defends itself against the muzhik, but the whole Church and city: "How did they not collapse—oh woe!—/How did they not leave their places,/The cross on the Kazan Cathedral/And the cross on St. Isaac's?/Over the awe-struck capital/Carry shots, shouts, the tocsin;/The city bares its teeth/Like a lioness defending her cubs." But the destruction of Rasputin is no resolution; if anything, it only intensifies the atmosphere of dread, since he is but one of so many:

"Well, go on, Orthodox folk, burn
My corpse on a dark bridge,
Scatter my ashes to the wind . . .
Who will defend me, an orphan?

In the wild and wretched land
There are many such muzhiks as I,
And the joyful rumble of their footsteps
Is heard along your roads."

In *The Pyre,* as in *The Quiver* and *The Tent,* poems on meta-physical themes and poems of fantasy, or of subjective, night-marish visions bordering on fantasy, are counterbalanced by poems in which the subject and treatment are basically realistic. The theme of Russia, while it is not quantitatively prominent in the book, is given three very different treatments: traditional fantasy ("The Serpent"); nightmare fantasy based on a real event ("The Muzhik"); and pseudorealistic ("Gorodok" [The Little Town, II, 7–8]). The latter is an evocation of the traditional atmosphere and way of life in a provincial Russian town. The town is not named, but it is characterized as "mentioned more than once by the chronicler." The contrast with "The Muzhik" could not be greater. Whereas that poem is pervaded with an atmosphere of dread, uncertainty, conflict, and instability, the atmosphere in "The Little Town" is one of calm, unquestioning confidence, and stability firmly rooted in tradition. The unspoken implication is that this is how life in the Russian provinces al-ways has been and always will be: "I know, that in this little town/Is genuine human life,/Like a little boat on a river,/ Headed for a known destination." In "The Muzhik," the Church is one of the institutions threatened by this bogus priest; in "The Little Town," the Church is one of the main repositories of the unshaken tradition. The poem may be termed "pseudo-realistic" because, although there are no elements of fantasy and the method is ostensibly realistic, with extensive use of realistic detail—"Striped posts at the guardhouse;" "All sorts of people at the bazaar:/Peasants, gypsies, itinerants"; "house-wives . . . in bright Samarkand kerchiefs"—the overall effect is that of a stylization, a dream of peace, rather than of a genre-scene or naturalism. This is partly due to the uniformly tranquil and positive tone, but not entirely. The poem is a word-picture, and the sort of picture it suggests to the reader's mind is a stylized miniature. Each of the stanzas, beginning with the third, presents a separate, enclosed little scene, and there is no attempt to provide transitions, to relate them other than by their presence within the same frame. The technique is reminiscent of medieval illuminations, with a variety of groups and activities presented on a single spatial plane. The sense of miniaturization is also contributed to by the frequent use of diminutives: the title itself (*gorodok*); little belt (*poiasok*), little boat (*lodochka*), etc. Particularly charming is the third stanza: "By the guardhouse, where little soldiers (*soldatiki*)/ March, veritable lunatics,/To the shrill wail of a trumpet" (the sound of a military trumpet is not normally "shrill," so sound as well as sight is subject to the diminishing effect).

The other three poems in *The Pyre*, besides a few of the love lyrics from the Blue Star cycle, that could be characterized as realistic are all personal lyrics, one looking to the poet's past ("Autumn"), one to his future ("The Workman"), and one to both past and future ("Ezbekiyeh").

"Osen'" (Autumn, II, 5; 95) is a scene from his childhood, describing how the boy Gumilev tried to catch an escaped horse. Unlike its companion piece "Detstvo" (Childhood, II, 6; 94), which quickly shifts from the sphere of earthly reality ("As a child I loved wide/Meadows that smelled of honey,/Copses, dry grasses") to the suprareal ("Each dusty roadside bush/Cried out to me, 'I'm fooling you,/Walk around me slowly/And you'll see what I really am!'"), "Autumn" remains firmly on the physical plane. Like "The Little Town," its method is pictorial, but whereas in that poem the painting is deliberately static, here it is vigorously dynamic. As Verkhovsky writes, "its pictorial quality is not merely external, but is so animated that, for example, it conveys with absolute immediacy that moment when the headlong motion suddenly stops—and, gasping for breath, you vacantly wonder at the motionless colors and vacantly listen to the wind, in which a moment before you were living, and straining, and rushing."[31] The reference is to the final lines:

> I'll have to sit down, I suppose,
> Out of breath, on a
> Wide flat stone,
> And wonder dully
> At the orange-red sky,
> And dully listen
> To the piercing cry of the wind.

The dynamic, spasmodic motion of the chase, by the way, is admirably conveyed by the shifting rhythms of the verse, an

unrhymed, unstanzaed *dol'nik* with irregular variations in anacrusis and number of stresses per line.

The realistic method and style of "Rabochii" (The Workman,
II, 14; 97)[32] stand in effective contrast to the poem's "prophetic"
subject. In this poem, one of his best known, Gumilev foresees
his own death in battle. The poem is sometimes considered literally prophetic—a premonition of Gumilev's execution. But as
the commentary to the poem in the Struve-Filippov edition
points out (II, 285), the reference is clearly to World War I.
The workman of the title is a German munitions-maker, and
Gumilev is foreseeing his death in combat. The poem was undoubtedly written while Gumilev was at the front.

Actually, the style of "The Workman" is not uniformly realistic:
it shifts in the middle, and this shift is an integral, calculated
feature of the poem's composition. The first half, three stanzas,
portrays a workman casting the bullet that is destined to kill
the poet, and is dense with commonplace realistic detail: "He
stands before a red-hot forge,/A short old man./His calm gaze
seems submissive/From the blinking of his reddish eyelids . . .
He finishes, and his eyes grow brighter./He returns. The moon
is shining./At home, a sleepy, warm wife/Awaits him in their
large bed." The second half portrays the poet's death, and there
is a definite shift in diction toward the abstract and the elevated:

> The bullet that he cast will whistle
> Over the grey-foaming Dvina,
> The bullet that he cast will seek out
> My breast, it has come for me.
>
> I will fall, seized by mortal grief,
> I will see my past before my eyes,
> My blood will gush like a spring
> Onto the dry, dusty, trampled grass.
>
> And the Lord will repay me in full measure
> For my brief and bitter span of years.
> And this was done by a short old man
> In a light-grey blouse.

The poem's central concern is of course the moment of death,
and the solemnity and significance of that moment cannot be

conveyed properly by purely physical detail. However, death is a physical as well as spiritual experience, and to treat it on a purely abstract plane would detract from the artistic impact. Gumilev solves this problem by the bipartite composition just described. As background to the moment of death, he provides the commonplace, homely scene of the workman going home to bed and wife after casting the fatal bullet, and the realistic force of this scene carries over, as it were, into the second part, so that the death scene is vividly concrete in spite of the more abstract diction of this part. Furthermore, the contrast between concrete and abstract is present within the second part as well as between the two parts. The moment of physical death is accompanied by the seemingly incidental detail of "dry, dusty, trampled grass," and the sentence conveying the metaphysical import of the moment ("And the Lord will repay me . . .") is followed by a sentence explicitly returning us to the beginning of the poem—with the addition of one more homely, incidental detail, the light grey blouse. The poem as a whole, then, provides an excellent example of the late Gumilev's mastery in combining the concrete realism of Acmeism with lyrical and metaphysical themes of great resonance, or as Verkhovsky puts it, "harmonious fusion of the ontological basis with the world of things, or, in other terms, of the spiritual-musical element with a chromatic-plastic perception of the sensible world."[33]

Verkhovsky here is referring specifically to the poem "Ez-bekiyeh" (II, 30–31),[34] which he considers a significant example of this sort of synthesis, as well as of the formal synthesis of the epic and lyric elements in Gumilev's poetry. "Ezbekiyeh," the final and longest piece in The Pyre (forty-five lines), tells of the poet's visit to the park of Ezbekiyeh in Cairo ten years previously, in 1907 ("How strange—exactly ten years have passed/ Since the last time when I saw Ezbekiyeh"), when, as he says, he "was tormented by a woman," and wanted to die: "I prayed to God for death then,/And was ready to hasten it myself." But the beauty of the park made him realize the value of life, and he made a vow to God that whatever suffering fell to his lot, he would not summon death before once more visiting Ezbekiyeh. Now that ten years have passed, his thoughts are full of Ezbekiyeh, and he feels he must return there and "renew

my vow/Or say that I have fulfilled it/And now am free. . . ."
The last line, "*I chto teper' svoboden . . .,*" is left incomplete,
but the word that obviously fits, both metrically and logically, is
umeret', to die. As Verkhovsky says, the poem is a fine synthesis
of various aspects of Gumilev's poetry: the narrative and the
lyrical, the concrete-descriptive and the abstract-metaphysical.
The passage describing the park is of particular interest: the
major physical features of the park are characterized in terms
of similes that are somewhat reminiscent of Gumilev's early
poetry in their abstractly decorative quality and whose function
is certainly less descriptive than atmospheric (to create an atmosphere of mystery, of the unearthly), but which still manage
to be visually evocative:

> But that garden in every way resembled
> The sacred groves of the earth's youth:
> There palm trees raised their slender branches
> Like maidens to whom God descends;
> On the hills, like oracular druids,
> Majestic plane trees clustered,
> And a waterfall gleamed white in the gloom,
> Like a rearing unicorn. . . .

A comparison of this poem with such earlier poems on the
theme of death as "Death" and "The Choice" from *Romantic
Flowers* shows how far Gumilev had come in ten years. The
abstract, decorative, rhetorical style and imagery have not been
abandoned, but they have been subjugated to a surer taste and
a firmer artistic hand, integrated with a more concretely descriptive element, and thereby given firmer roots in earthly reality
and in the poet's individual spiritual experience. His poetry no
longer conveys an atmosphere of free-floating, impersonalized
fantasy and imagination, but rather of the inner world of a
highly individual artist, endowed with sensual perceptiveness,
spiritual sensitivity, and the ability to convey his emotional pain
and joy and his metaphysical insights in plastic and universally
accessible terms.

IV Pillar of Fire

Pillar of Fire, Gumilev's last book, is also by general critical
consensus his best and most significant. It is one of his smaller

books of poetry: it consists of nineteen lyrics totaling less than 700 lines, and one longish narrative poem ("Stellar Terror," 195 lines). Whereas *The Pyre* consisted mainly of rather short poems, in the range of four to six quatrains, those in *Pillar of Fire* are generally longer. Even excluding "Stellar Terror," ten of the poems are thirty lines or longer, and five are over fifty lines in length. This is a matter of more than merely statistical interest; it is one reflection of clear, overall difference in tone between the two. The general tone in *The Pyre* tends toward the intimately personal, partly but not entirely because of the prominence of the love theme. The poetic subjects are for the most part such as can be adequately, and most appropriately, treated in a few stanzas. In *Pillar of Fire*, the meditative and rhetorical elements are much stronger, and the subjects in many cases seem to require a somewhat ampler form. This does not mean that the poetry is no longer lyrical. It is still intensely personal, but personal in a different way, less intimately and more complexly personal. It is as if the poet were striving, in an individual poem, not so much toward a maximally intense expression of a single lyrical emotion or idea, as for example in "Childhood," from *The Pyre*, as toward a comprehensive expression of a whole range or set of emotions and ideas. Two of the most personal poems in *Pillar of Fire*, "Memory" and "The Streetcar Gone Astray," are also two of the longest and most complex. It is noteworthy that the titles of both books have to do with fire. While it might be reading into the titles meanings that the author did not intend, one might take the titles as an indication of the difference in lyrical stance between the two books. In *The Pyre*, the poet is presenting himself as a romantic idealist, as Lover, ready to mount the pyre of love and there either be destroyed, or be purged of the dross of earthly existence and thus be prepared to live in the realm of the Ideal. In *Pillar of Fire*, he is still an idealist, still a lover, but now above all a Poet, specifically in the Romantic ideal of Poet as Prophet, with the vision that enables him to see that pillar of fire that the ordinary mortal cannot see, and hence the duty to lead his people where the pillar leads him: along the path to the Ideal. The destination is the same, but in *The Pyre* it is purely personal, whereas in *Pillar of Fire* it is at once personal and collective.

This idea of the poet's mission is developed explicitly in "Pamiat'" (Memory, II, 35–37; 109–10):[35]

> I am the somber, stubborn builder
> Of a temple that rises in the gloom,
> I have devoted myself to the Father's glory,
> On earth, as in Heaven.
>
> My heart will be seared by flame
> Until the day when the bright walls
> Of the new Jerusalem rise up
> On the fields of my native land.

"Memory" is the opening poem of *Pillar of Fire*, and this placement is clearly deliberate. This piece, in form a sort of retrospective spiritual diary, introduces most of the major themes of the book: the poet's own life-experience; religion and metaphysics; poetry. The only major theme of the book that does not appear here is that of love.

In "Memory" Gumilev takes us through several stages of his life: three or four past stages (the poet himself is uncertain of the number, as we shall see), the present stage, and a future stage. The idea of a poetic summation and evaluation of one's past life is of course not new. However, Gumilev formulates the theme with a touch of originality by means of the concept of "changing souls," that is, of several different "souls" (personalities) inhabiting in turn the same body, to which he contrasts the snake's habit of shedding its skin: "Only snakes shed their skins . . . We change our souls, not our bodies." These phrases recur at the beginning and end, giving the poem a circular construction. They comprise the first and last lines of the opening quatrain and the last two lines of the closing one.

The first "soul" to inhabit Gumilev's body was the lonely dreamer of his childhood:

> The very first was homely and thin,
> He loved only the twilight of forest groves,
> And fallen leaves; he was a wizard-child,
> Who would stop the rain with a word.

> A tree and a red-haired dog
> Were all he took as friends;
> Memory, Memory, you won't find a sign,
> You'll not convince the world that that was I.

This section (stanzas 3 and 4) echoes "Autumn" and "Childhood" from *The Pyre* ("shaggy and red, my dog . . . who is dearer to me than even my own brother . . ." II, 5; and "As a child, I loved wide/Meadows that smelled of honey,/ Copses, dry grasses . . ." II, 6). The obvious interpretation of the phrase "a wizard-child,/Who would stop the rain with a word"—that the child lived in a world of the imagination—finds its confirmation in a passage from Odoevsteva's memoirs: " 'My childhood was strangely magical,' he told me. 'I really was a wizard-child. I lived in a world that I created myself, not understanding yet that it was the world of poetry. . . . In the evenings I would lock my door, stand in front of the mirror and hypnotize myself into becoming handsome. I firmly believed that I could change my appearance by strength of will.' "[36]

The second soul, that of the poet in stanzas 5 and 6, is the one, strangely, that appeals least to the present Gumilev, while his favorite is the third, the hunter-explorer of stanzas 7 and 8. This personality is obviously closely related to the one who volunteered for combat in World War I (stanzas 9 and 10), and Gumilev himself is not sure whether they are separate stages ("Was it he, or another one/Who exchanged his joyous freedom/For the sacred, long-awaited battle"). What is significant here is not the similarity between these two souls, but the possibility of their separation, for while in one sense his military service was only an extension of the desire for adventure and challenge that took him to Africa, in another sense the war experience seems to have been a significant landmark in his spiritual growth, as indicated by the greater psychological complexity and philosophical depth of his postwar poetry. This is expressed in the poem by the sudden shift from the war stanzas to an unmediated expression of the major concern of the "present" Gumilev—his sense of a religious mission, in stanzas 11 and 12, quoted above. The image in stanza 11 of the building of a temple as a metaphor for a spiritual feat had appeared earlier, in "The Middle Ages" (*The Quiver*) and in the first version of that natural companion-piece to "Memory," "Iambic Pentameters." In both the earlier poems the source of the metaphor in Masonic imagery is made explicit.

The completion of the religious mission will bring about the final, future stage, which is one of entry into a transcendent reality, as indicated by the apocalyptic tone and the allusions to Revelation:

> And then a strange wind will rise—
> And an awesome light will spill from heaven:
> The Milky Way blossoming unexpectedly,
> A garden of dazzling planets.
>
> An unknown traveller will appear before me,
> His face hidden; but I'll understand it all
> When I see the lion racing at his heels,
> And the eagle flying to him.[37]

The poem then closes with the repetition of the formula from the first stanza. However, at its second appearance the formula takes on a new resonance. It now serves to emphasize the finality of the last stage, for once the soul has been confronted by the Christ of the Apocalypse, no further change is possible: "I shall cry out . . . But will anyone help/To save my soul from death?/Only snakes. . . ."

Space does not allow a discussion here of the nature and content of the religious mission that Gumilev mentions in "Memory," and his other poetry offers precious little toward such a discussion. But independent of its nature, its very existence is significant, for we can see Gumilev here seeking still another field for heroic exploits, for the "pathos of endeavor." In speaking of the first soul, the child, he had said, "Memory, Memory, you won't find a sign,/You'll not convince the world that that was I." Yet there is a "sign," a link between all the stages: the Superman impulse, the desire for experience and achievement beyond the reach of ordinary human beings. The child is a "wizard-child"; the poet "wanted to become a god and a tsar"; the explorer is envied by the clouds, and the waters sing to him; and the "builder" is going to bring about the Millennium.

"Zabludivshiisia tramvai" (The Streetcar Gone Astray, II, 48–50; 105–106),[38] like "Memory," is a poem that looks at the poet's past and into his future. But aside from this thematic similarity, the poems are very different. "Memory" is relatively simple and straightforward in its revelation of the poet's inner world. The expression is metaphorical, but the images are uncomplicated, logical in themselves and in their relation to one another. The composition is logical, too, moving chronologically through the stages of the poet's life. "The Streetcar Gone Astray" is quite another matter. The images are more obscure and puzzling, the composition involuted; it displays a continual shifting and interplay of temporal and spatial planes, which have led various commentators to call the poem "surrealistic." That term also conveys the dreamlike atmosphere of the poem: "The Streetcar" is another of those nightmare visions that recur throughout Gumilev's poetry, but with increasing frequency, vividness, force, and psychological reality in his last period. But the terms "dream" and "nightmare" mean more in regard to this poem than the quality of individual images and the apparent disorder in their interrelationships. They imply also the poem's roots in the irrational, subconscious levels of the poet's mind, its nature as a poetic vision, not just a transcription of conscious experience into metrical and metaphorical speech. The very nature of the imagery in this poem differs from that in "Memory." Take, for instance, the central organizing images of the two poems: the "changing of souls" in the one, and the streetcar in the other. The former is definitely a cerebral image; it is a metaphor, no more, and the poet, like a good Acmeist, has it under his conscious control, not allowing it to overstep its bounds, but using it to help him organize his perception of reality. In "The Streetcar," on the other hand, the metaphor has control of the poet, as it were, leading his consciousness at will. Metaphor and reality became inextricably intertwined; this can happen because the reality of the poem is not the reality of the everyday rational consciousness, but a deeper inner reality. Odoevtseva gives a fascinating report of Gumilev's account of the poem's creation:

> I don't understand even now how it happened. I was crossing a bridge over the Neva.... The place was deserted; only crows were cawing. And suddenly a streetcar flew by me, very close. Its sparks were like a fiery path against the rosy dawn. I stopped. Something suddenly penetrated me. . . . I seemed to remember something in the distant past, and at the same time seemed to see the future. But it was all very vague and oppressive. I looked around, not understanding where I was and what was happening to me ... then I slowly moved on. And then it happened. I immediately found the first stanza, as though I received it complete, and didn't compose it myself.... I continued walking and speaking line after line, as though I were reciting someone else's poem. The whole thing, right to the end.[39]

The difference in atmosphere between the two poems is emphasized by the difference in meter. "Memory" is written in regular syllabo-tonic verse (trochaic pentameter); "The Streetcar" is in a four-stress *dol'nik* line on a dactylic base (i.e. with a zero anacrusis), a form of *dol'nik* unusual for Gumilev. The greater rhythmical freedom and variety of the *dol'nik*, as compared to syllabo-tonic verse, is in harmony with the atmosphere of the poem.

Despite its apparent lack of logic and order, the composition of the poem has its own logic, the key to which is found in the third stanza: "It went astray in the abyss of time," reminiscent of the lines from "Stockholm": "I was lost for aye/ In the blind passages of space and time." The streetcar has jumped the tracks of chronological time, and is free to cross at will between past, present, and future. First it carries the poet into his past, and crosses in rapid succession the three rivers that have been an important part of that past:

> Stop, driver,
> Stop the car at once.
>
> Too late. We've already skirted the wall,
> We've flown through a palm grove,

We've thundered over three bridges,
Across the Neva, across the Nile, and the Seine.

And, flashing past the window frame,
An old beggar cast a searching glance
After us—of course, he's the same
Who died in Beirut a year ago.

At this point, the poet realizes that he has left the normal space-time continuum, and thus other levels of reality are open to him: "Where am I? So pained and troubled,/My heart beats in answer:/Do you see the station where one can buy/A ticket to the India of the Spirit?" Next, a brief foray into the future, where the poet sees himself beheaded, contains the most grotesquely nightmarish images in the whole poem:

A sign . . . letters suffused with blood
Proclaim: Greengrocers—here, I know,
Instead of cabbage, instead of rutabagas,
Lifeless heads are sold.

In a red shirt, with a face like an udder,
The executioner cut off my head as well;
It lay together with the others
Here in a slippery box, on the very bottom.

The poet is then carried back into another part of the past, and full of horror as the preceding passage was, his alarm is apparently now even greater. When he realizes where the streetcar has taken him now, he repeats his appeal to the driver to stop, and this time more insistently: there is an exclamation mark, where there was none before:

And in a side street, a wooden fence,
A house with three windows and a grey lawn . . .
Stop, driver,
Stop the car at once!

Mashenka, you lived here and sang here,
And wove a rug for me, your betrothed,
Where are your voice and body now,
Can it be that you have died!

> How you moaned in your parlor,
> While I, with a powdered queue,
> Went to present myself to the Empress,
> And I never saw you again.

The temporal relationships have become even more intricate, for the poet has apparently been carried outside his own personal past. The phrases "powdered queue" and "to present myself to the Empress" and the archaism *svetlitsa* (parlor) suggest the eighteenth century. Perhaps it is the past of an ancestor, or an earlier incarnation—the idea of memory of a former existence or of a racial past occurs several times in Gumilev. It is unclear, and the ambiguity is no doubt deliberate, whether the Mashenka of this episode is intended to have any relationship to the poet's "real" past, though her reappearance in the last stanza implies that she does. The alarm expressed by the repetition of the appeal to the driver may stem from the poet's realization that the errant streetcar has broken through not only the boundaries between his past, present, and future, but those between his own past and a more distant one. He has lost the security of knowing the limits of his own past and memories, as they become inexplicably and irrevocably intertwined with other pasts, other memories. Incidentally, some of Gumilev's associates have seen a literal biographical significance in the name Mashenka, while Odoevtseva's account of the writing of the poem indicates that the choice of name was more or less fortuitous.[40] Whatever Gumilev's reasons for using the name, we understand the poem better if we do not try to associate Mashenka with anyone in his biography. She is not any individual woman, but an image of the ideal love that he had sought throughout his life and poetry.

This second excursion into the past is followed by an expression of the insight to which this crisscrossing of temporal planes has brought the poet: "Now I understand: our freedom/Is only the light that strikes from there,/People and shades stand at the entrance/To the zoological garden of the planets." That is, what seems to us our freedom—to act according to our will, to arrange our fates—is really only a light from beyond, the light of the fire of Plato's cave. "People" (inhabitants of this world, the physical universe) and "shades" (the dead and the not-yet-born) are not the separate entities that they seem from the earthly perspective; in the realm of the true reality, they are on an equal footing.

This insight brings the streetcar's trip to an end and returns the poet to the present place and time:

> And immediately a sweet, familiar wind,
> And beyond the bridge, flying toward me—
> The Horseman's palm in its iron glove
> And the two hooves of his horse.

> The true bastion of Orthodoxy,
> St. Isaac's is etched on the sky,
> There I will attend a mass for Mashenka's
> Health, and a Requiem for myself.

But the temporal planes are still not completely sorted out, for the poet is going to attend a service for the health of the dead Mashenka and a requiem Mass for himself. The details of the scene to which the poet returns after his excursion through time are a masterly combination of concrete precision and symbolic significance, and as such may serve as an archetypical example of the tendencies of the mature Gumilev's art. These details are chosen so as to define quite precisely the physical perspective. Approaching the Bronze Horseman—Falconet's equestrian statue of Peter the Great in St. Petersburg—from the left, one sees the dominant details as the Tsar's outstretched right hand and his horse's raised front hooves, with the dome of the Cathedral of St. Isaac against the sky in the background. At the same time, they indicate the poet's return to his two major extrapersonal concerns in the present: the fate of Russia, symbolized by the statue of Peter the Great, and the fate of Orthodoxy. These are followed immediately by his two main personal concerns, his ideal love and his own fate. The last stanza ends the poem on a note of searing emotional pain:

> And still my heart is forever dark,
> And it's difficult to breathe, and painful to live . . .
> Mashenka, I never believed
> It possible so to love and grieve.

I have analyzed these two poems at some length because they seem to me to be central to the collection and to a complete image of the mature Gumilev, in terms of both poetic technique and content. "Memory" exemplifies the essentially Acmeistic technique of the bulk of Gumilev's earlier work, while using that technique to express ideological concerns somewhat at variance with the conventional image of Gumilev the Acmeist. "The Streetcar" exemplifies the more complex, denser style toward which he seemed to be moving. The two together embrace all of the major themes of the book: the poet's own life experience, including his past adventures and his future fate; religion and metaphysics; poetry; and love.

"The Streetcar Gone Astray" is the most remarkable poem in the book, and perhaps in all of Gumilev's work. However, it does not stand isolated. There are several other poems in *Pillar of Fire* that are similar in style and technique, and while there are also poems that are very different, the general tendency and tone of the book is set not by them, but by such poems as "The Streetcar," "Among the Gypsies," "The Forest," "The Bird-Maiden," and "Soul and Body." "The Streetcar," then, is just the most fully elaborated example of what seems to have been the beginning of a new departure in the poet's development, a development broken off prematurely by his execution. It must of course remain a matter of speculation as to whether this new trend would have led him to still greater poetic achievements, but the promise is certainly present in *Pillar of Fire*.

The poem most closely related to "The Streetcar" by its complex style and technique is "U tsygan" (Among the Gypsies, II, 51–53), which, however, is less radically surrealistic and seems to hover about the point at which radical impressionism passes over into surrealism. The poem operates on two levels: the "realistic" level of a scene in a gypsy tavern involving a drunken hussar who, inflamed by a gypsy dancer, dances himself into a frenzy and eventually into unconsciousness; and the second level, of the poetic-nightmarish visions that the scene evokes in the poet-spectator:

> A string . . . and a throaty howl . . . and immediately
> Such a sweet ache in my blood,

So earnestly did I believe the tale
Of another land, a land where I was born.

The vatic strings are oxen's tendons
But these oxen fed on bitter grass,
. . . .
There are strings-oxen to the right and to the left,
Their horns are death, and their bellowing is woe,
There are bitter grasses on their pastures:
Thorny thistles, wormwood, goose-foot.

These visions carry the poet out of the tavern into a more
rustic scene: "The flame of a bonfire, the flame of a bonfire,
columns/Of red trunks, and a deafening yell,/The enamored
guest tramples rust-red leaves,/A Bengal tiger whirling in the
crowd." But they also carry him further, onto another level
of existence:

Is it for me to see him [the hussar—E.S.] in clouds of cigar smoke,
Where corks pop and people shout,
Rapping out the tempo of his evil heart
On a wet table, with an amber pipe?

Me, who remembers him in a barque of diamonds,
On a river that courses toward God,
The dread of angels, and a sweet temptation,
With a bloody lily in his slender hand?

This image is so sharply at variance with the initial image of
the drunken officer given in the first stanza ("Hulking, he swayed
as if in a trance,/His teeth glistened under his ferocious mus-
tache,/The knots of his gold braid intertwined/On his bright-red
dolman") that we can only conclude that the poet-spectator is
merging his own soul with that of the hussar. Vicariously ex-
periencing the dancer's passion, he imputes to him the same
sense of a higher existence that he, the poet, experiences under
the influence of passion, and even the same realization of the
ambiguity inherent in a transcendent experience that has its
roots in sensual passion (a *bloody* lily).
The poem's two levels are separable only upon analysis; in

the text of the poem itself, they are tightly intertwined. Thus, for example, just before the hussar collapses, he is said to have been stabbed in the heart by a piece of "jagged flint." The next lines, in their prosaic tone, would seem to imply that this took place only in the poet's imagination, as an actualization of a metaphor ("struck to the heart"):

> He crashed to the floor, his aiguillettes tangled,
> We no longer care to drink, or watch,
> The waiters bustled about,
> Carrying away the drunken client.
>
> Well, gentlemen, so it's five-thirty?
> Bring us our check, Asmodeus!

But then the poem ends with two lines that place the relationship between imagination and reality again in doubt: "The girl, laughing, with her narrow tongue/Licks the blood from the strip of flint."

Alongside the highly subjective nightmare visions of "The Streetcar" and "Among the Gypsies," there are poems in *Pillar of Fire* in which the fantasy is much more stylized and channeled, drawing on more traditional motifs. In particular there are two stylized ballads: "Persten'" (The Ring), in which a girl drops her ring down a well, and entreats the inhabitants of the well—"tritons and wet undines"—to return it to her; and the more substantial "Deva-ptitsa" (The Bird Maiden, II, 58–60; 113–15).

The tradition on which Gumilev draws for "The Bird-Maiden" is that of the tales of the Knights of the Round Table. The setting is the land of Broceliande, and the atmosphere of the poem is that of a medieval fairy-tale, very skillfully evoked. The content, however, is Gumilev's own, expressing his own outlook. The ballad relates an encounter between a young cowherd and a fabulous creature, "a flamelike bird,/With the head of a fair maiden." When he wonders at her mournful song, she explains that she is fated to live without a mate:

> "There is none like unto me
> On the green earth.

> And although a bird-lad
> Full of wondrous desires,
> Is to be born
> In Broceliande,
>
> But an evil
> Fate denies us pleasure,
> Only think, cowherd, I must
> Die before he is born.
>
> And so I take no pleasure
> Nor in the sun, nor in the moon on high,
> No one needs my lips
> And my pale cheeks."

And the bird-lad, when he is born, will also be sad: he will perch on these very elms and call for a lady-love who no longer lives. And so she asks the cowherd to caress her, so that he will remember her and tell his children of her, and thus her memory will be passed on to future ages. He approaches, and is overcome by passion: "Now he is in a frenzy,/He knows not himself what he does,/His sunburned knees/Crush the red feathers./Only once did the bird moan,/She moaned but once,/And the heart in her breast/Suddenly ceased beating." The cowherd then plays mournful songs over her on his reed-pipe, in contrast to the "song of joys" that he played before the encounter, and at evenfall drives his herd home. Here the ballad ends, and the future—the fate of the bird-maiden's memory and the fate of the bird-lad—is left for another, unwritten ballad.

The poem may be, as Sergey Makovsky characterizes it, "a complex cryptogram in the Romantic-Maeterlinckian style," but aside from any difficulty of interpretation of individual symbolic details, the central idea seems to be quite clear: it is another treatment of Gumilev's frequent theme of Ideal Love and its inspirative and transfiguring influence on the poet. The cowherd is both the lover and the poet, whose songs are changed by the encounter from gay (worldly) to mournful (spiritual), and the bird-lad (also a singer) is his future incarnation, his spiritual essence. The bird-maiden is both Ideal Woman and Muse, whom, as Makovsky says, he does not recognize in his incarnation as cowherd because "he met her before he was 'born' as a visionary poet, while still only light-heartedly singing his 'song of joys.' In the vales of Broceliande he only instinctively yields to her charms, and 'knows not himself what he does' when he kills her with a kiss. But the bird he has killed will summon him from the other, transfigured world.... She is, in fact, Gumilev's true Muse; his inner poetic essence is nowhere so well expressed as in the poems of a love that brings his soul in contact with the eternal. It was thus from his first steps in poetry, from his youthful verses."[41]

The death of the bird is a troublesome detail. Does it signify the deadening effect on ideal concepts of the attempt to fix them into poetic form, or the corruption of ideal love through its corporeal expression, or both, or something else again? In any case, the central idea is clear enough, and the central images and their underlying meanings are part of Gumilev's established poetic system.

Other love poems in the book also emphasize love as a link between the two levels of existence; for example "Les" (The Forest, II, 37–38; 111–12):[42] "Perhaps that forest is your soul,/ Perhaps that forest is my love,/ Or, perhaps, when we die,/You and I will go together to that forest"; "P'ianyi dervish" (The Drunken Dervish, II, 53–54; 122): "The world is but a ray from my beloved's countenance, all else is its shadow!"; and "Canzonet Two" (II, 43–44; 120):

> And only in your secret sorrow,
> My love, is there a burning, numbing intoxication,
> That in this accursed, God-forsaken place
> Is like a wind out of distant lands.
>
> There, where all is lustre, all is motion,
> All is song—there live you and I.
> While here the foul pond
> Captures only our reflection.

One of the more prominent themes in *Pillar of Fire* is the theme of poetry itself, poetic creation or artistic creation in general; it is perhaps second only to the love theme. Perhaps this reflects the poet's consciousness of an incipient change in the nature of his poetry, since the theme is more pronounced here

than in any of the earlier books, for it is a central subject of
several poems, and an important subtheme in several others.
Probably the most significant of these is "Slovo" (The Word,
II, 39; 107),[43] in which Gumilev speaks of the power over
matter that the word once possessed: "In those days, when God
bent His face/Over the newborn world, then/The sun could
be stopped by a word,/The word could destroy cities./And the
eagle closed his wings,/Stars pressed in terror to the moon,/If
the word, like a rosy flame,/Sailed across the heavens" and contrasts this with its present-day subordinate position:

> But we have forgotten, that among our earthly cares,
> Only the word is luminous,
> And in the Gospel according to St. John
> It is said that the word is God.
>
> We have set it limits—
> The meager limits of substantiality,
> And, like bees in an abandoned hive,
> Dead words emit an evil smell.

These do not sound like the words of an Acmeist, to be sure. But
Gumilev always knew that the reach of the poetic word cannot
be limited to the world of substance, and he never tried so to
limit it, even at the height of his campaign against the Symbolists'
tendency to overextend that reach. On the other hand, the poetry
of *Pillar of Fire* is very different from that of *Foreign Skies,* and
this change in poetic practice is inevitably associated with some
changes in Gumilev's attitudes toward the poetic word and the
task of the poet, changes partially expressed in "The Word" and
in "Shestoe chuvstvo" (The Sixth Sense, II, 46–47; 116).[44] The
stance of the latter poem is also somewhat at odds with Acmeism's
putative concern with the corporeal:

> Fine is the wine that loves us
> And the goodly bread that for us goes in the oven,
> And woman, given to us
> First for torment, then for pleasure.
>
> But what are we to do with the rosy glow
> Over gradually cooling skies

> Wherein is silence and unearthly calm,
> What are we to do with immortal verse?
>
> They cannot be eaten, drunk, nor kissed.
> The moment flits inexorably by,
> And we wring our hands, but still and again
> We're fated to miss the mark, to miss the mark.
>
> . . . .
>
> . . . age after age—will it be soon, oh Lord?—
> Under the scalpel of nature and of art,
> Our spirit cries out, our flesh faints,
> Bringing forth an organ for the sixth sense.

In his Acmeist manifesto, Gumilev had written: "To keep in mind always the unknowable, but not offend one's thoughts about it with more or less likely conjectures—this is the principle of Acmeism. This does not mean that we relinquish the right to show the soul trembling as it approaches the Other; but at such moments it should shudder, and no more than that" (IV, 175). It could be argued that Gumilev had never submitted himself entirely to such a limitation, but what "The Sixth Sense" seems to express is an open abandonment of the position. The poet may still be fated "to miss the mark, to miss the mark" (*idti vse mimo, mimo*), but he is no longer willing to do so deliberately, nor passively to accept the limitation. Now he aims actively to enlist his art in the task of "bringing forth an organ for the sixth sense," or, to use Verkhovsky's formulation for the interpretation of that image, the task of expressing that which "was revealed to the poet beyond the world of things—their noumenal essence."[45]

While the thematics of *Pillar of Fire* are rather varied, as a whole the book displays more unity of tone than perhaps any of Gumilev's other collections. This unity stems to a great extent from the metaphysical element present in such differing poems as "Memory," "The Streetcar Gone Astray," "The Word," "The Forest," "Canzonet Two," "Among the Gypsies," "The Drunken Dervish," and "The Bird-Maiden." In this sense, one of the book's central poems is the explicitly metaphysical "Dusha i telo" (Soul and Body, II, 40–42; 117–18). The poem is divided into three parts of five quatrains each. In the first part, the soul complains, in fairly conventional terms, of its thraldom to the physical: "Why did I open my eyes to existence/In a paltry human body?/Recklessly I abandoned my home,/Striving for a different sort of grandeur./And the orb of earth has become for me the ball/To which a prisoner is shackled by a chain." In the second part, the body responds that it knows not what "existence" is, but it knows what love is, what the physical pleasures are, and it also knows and accepts the ineluctable limits and conditions of physical existence:

> But I know what they call love.
>
> I love to splash in a briny wave,
> To listen to the cries of hawks,
> I love to race on an unbroken horse
> Over a meadow that smells of caraway.
>
> And I love woman . . .
> . . . .
>
> But for all that I have taken, and still desire,
> For all my sorrows, joys, and frenzies,
> I will pay, as befits a real man
> With the final, irreversible extinction.

This sort of contraposition of the soul and body occurs elsewhere in Gumilev—for instance, in "A Conversation" from *The Quiver*—as indeed in many other Romantic poets. But the interesting, original part of the poem is the third part, where the poet himself speaks as a sort of essential ego that transcends both soul and body, and whose ultimate origin goes far beyond the cosmos in which those two exist:

> But when the word of God from on high
> Blazed forth in the form of Ursa Major
> With the question, "And who, inquisitor, are you?"
> My soul and body stood before me.
>
> I slowly fixed my gaze on them
> And gave indulgent reply to their audacity:
> "Tell me, is a dog then rational
> If he howls when the moon shines?

Is it then for you to question me,
Me for whom the entire term
From earth's first day to the fiery Apocalypse
Is but a single moment?

Me, whose stature, like Yggdrasill,
Towers over seven times seven universes,
And in whose eyes the fields of earth
And even the Elysian Fields are but motes of dust?

I am the one who sleeps, and the deeps
Conceal my unutterable name!
But you, you are but the feeble reflection of a dream
Flickering in the depths of my consciousness!"

One wants to be cautious in applying the term "metaphysical" to such a poem. We could, certainly, extrapolate from it the outlines of a rather extravagant metaphysic, but this would be at variance with the poet's intent. The poem's images, particularly in the third part, are strictly poetic images, a hyperbolic expression of the poet's sense of an essential, indestructible core of being within himself, so absolutely eternal and indestructible that even the imagery of Christian eschatology and cosmology is not sufficient to express it. In other words, religious convictions are not the issue in this poem, which is perhaps the most forceful expression of one of Gumilev's essential beliefs, one which is put forth in many other poems via a wide variety of means of expression—the belief in the absolute value of the individual consciousness. And this concern with individual consciousness could be extended to embrace a much wider range of Gumilev's poetry—virtually all of it—if we add that for Gumilev individual consciousness is a dynamic concept, it implies not merely passive perception, but action. It is for him virtually synonymous with individual will, and if there is one central underlying theme in his whole body of poetry and indeed in his whole life, it is this: to express your will, to translate your will into action, to impose your will on the world, no matter what the obstacles or consequences.[46]

The central significance of *Pillar of Fire* in Gumilev's *oeuvre* stems not only from the sustained high level of poetic achievement, but also from the collection's relationship to his other books, especially those of his mature period, 1913–1921. That relationship is twofold, for *Pillar of Fire* is at once a culmination and a new departure. Its links with the earlier work are organic in that it brings to full fruition certain lines of development discernible in the preceding years, in the spheres of both subject matter and artistic technique. On the other hand, it stands apart in its unique unity of tone and theme. This unity results from the choices Gumilev has made from among the various possibilities inherent in his earlier work. Some of them have been abandoned; thus, the image of the poet-warrior is absent from the book, with the exception of "My Readers"; the line of Acmeist technique, narrowly understood, has also been discarded. In their place, Gumilev has emphasized themes and motifs of nightmarish fantasy, of "sorcery and witchcraft" (from a line in "The Leopard"), of religion, and visions of a transcendental reality. Furthermore, he has intensified such motifs, and the means of poetic expression appropriate to them, to the point of heralding a "new Gumilev," an essentially different kind of poetry.

This trend of development has led a number of critics to speak of a "return to Symbolism" in the late Gumilev. This formula has considerable validity, but like all such conveniently brief formulas it can also be misleading if not properly qualified. Above all, it should not be taken to imply any sort of regression, any return to the sort of poetry the youthful Gumilev wrote under the influence of his early Symbolist masters, or the sort of poetry those masters themselves wrote in the first decade or so of the century. The naive, imitative "Symbolism" of *The Path of Conquistadors* and *Romantic Flowers* is poles apart from the vigorous, original, much more profound symbolism of *Pillar of Fire*,[47] just as the fantasy of the early poetry has virtually nothing in common with the fantasy of *The Pyre, The Tent*, or *Pillar of Fire*, or, to some extent, even *The Quiver* and *Foreign Skies*. If there is a return, it is a return on another, higher level of the spiral, as Vladimir Nabokov uses the image of the spiral in his reminiscences, *Speak, Memory*, and elsewhere. Verkhovsky sums up the development with the rather ponderous but still accurate formulations of Vyacheslav Ivanov:

And so—into what sphere of art, by what path, does the Muse of Distant Travels lead her poet? We have already used the word: Symbolist. Yes, Symbolism, as a path. The symbolism, not of a school, but of a Weltanschauung, of an artistic world-perception and of poetic creation.... We find in Vyacheslav Ivanov's "The Precepts of Symbolism"... the definition of the two characteristic features of a purely Symbolistic art (we quote in extract): "1) a parallelism, consciously expressed by the artist, between the phenomenal and the noumenal; a harmoniously discovered consonance of realia and realioria; an indication of the correspondences and correlations between the phenomenon ... and its intellectually perceived essence. 2) A special intuition and energy of the *word*, which is directly sensed by the poet as a cryptogram of the unspoken, and which gathers up into its sound many echos, resounding from who knows whence, and serves as the letters of the outer experience and the hieroglyphs of the inner." And do we not find both, at least in the form of a powerful tendency, in Gumilev's poetry?[48]

To which it might be added that, if the late Gumilev came to Symbolism, he did after all come to it through Acmeism and from an earlier stage of Symbolist influence, so that the image of the spiral is appropriate. He returned to "Symbolism" enriched by a strict self-schooling in poetic technique and by an extensive, complex, contradictory, and often painful spiritual odyssey. And it was this artistic discipline, this profoundly assimilated spiritual experience, that lent Gumilev's last poems their enduring artistic significance.

CHAPTER 5

Narrative and Dramatic Poetry

I *Narrative Poetry*

THERE is no clear-cut division within Gumilev's poetry between the narrative and lyrical modes. As Verkhovsky emphasizes, there is a strong "lyro-epic" strain running throughout his poetry, which finds a variety of modes of expression. In the poems that may be thus characterized, there is a wide variation in the degree of emphasis given to the lyrical or the narrative component, ranging from the highly personal lyricism of "Iambic Pentameters" to such a poem as "Discovery of America," with its strong narrative structure and its more indirect lyricism; the many "little ballads" that constitute a major portion of *Romantic Flowers* and *Pearls* show a similar variation in emphasis. There are also a few poems more strictly in the epic, rather than lyro-epic, mode, such as *Mik*.

Nonetheless, I have chosen to treat separately Gumilev's major narrative poems, those that with more or less justification can be designated as *poemy*—the Russian genre term for longer poetic works of a primarily narrative nature[1]—mainly in order to emphasize the justification for making such a genre distinction within Gumilev's *oeuvre*: that despite the very close links between the lyric and the epic, and the presence of poems of a mixed or transitional nature, there does exist a separate or separable epic mode that, while definitely secondary in importance to the lyric mode, is pronounced enough to deserve a modicum of separate attention. Gumilev's own treatment of his *poemy* within his published collections indicates that he himself lent the distinction some importance, for as a rule the *poemy* are placed at the end of the books.

Gumilev's earliest *poemy*, besides those in *The Path of Conquistadors*, were "Neo-Romantic Fairy Tale," "The Northern

Rajah," and "Adam's Dream," all included in the 1910 edition
of *Pearls*. The first two may be dismissed briefly. "Neo-Romantic
Fairy-Tale" (I, 87–89) is a stylized ballad, a slight piece done
entirely in a lighthearted vein. "The Northern Rajah" (I, 278–82)
is more serious in intent but less successful in execution. It is
a rather clumsy advocacy of the claims of the artistic imagination, and Gumilev was correct in deleting the piece when he
revised *Pearls* in 1918.

"Adam's Dream" (I, 147–51), on the other hand, is a more
ambitious and a more successful effort. Written in amphibrachic
tetrameter sextets, it presents the history of mankind, from
the expulsion from Eden to Judgment Day, in the form of a
dream dreamt by Adam before the Serpent's temptation. This is a
rather bold endeavor to try to encompass in the space of 108
lines, and it is remarkable how well the twenty-four-year-old
poet succeeded. There is no attempt to embrace specific historical events and landmarks, but mankind's primary fields
of endeavor and of spiritual struggle are vividly evoked in
compact images:

> He curbed the flow of the violent torrent,
> By sleepless thought he fathomed equilibrium,
> Like a hawk he soars into the skies,
> From the stubborn earth he wrests ores.
> Submissive and silent, books preserve for him
> The melodies of poets and the secrets of faith.
>
> . . . .
>
> He loves the sport of dangerous games:
> To seek out unknown lands in the oceans,
> To set reckless foot in wolf-haunted glades,
> And to see the plain from high mountains.
>
> . . . .
>
> He loves also the scrape of the steel chisel
> That splinters lumpish marble into a statue,
> And the chaste cold of a rosy dawn,
> And the tender oval of a young face,—
> When they take shape bright and radiant,
> Under the strokes of the brush on canvas.
>
> . . . .

> He continually expects from the rosy distance
> New thoughts, like radiant guests,
> And with them, like new stars, the sorrows
> Of hitherto unknown thoughts and passions,
> Failures of dreams and terror in art,
> Making the heart ache from grievous forebodings.

Another major motif of the poem, an elaboration of Genesis
3:15 ("And I will put enmity between thee and the woman, and
between thy seed and her seed"), is the relationship through
the ages between man and woman. Immediately after the expulsion, "now for the first time he comprehended unity with
a woman. / To her—the bliss and pain of motherhood, / To him—
a spade, to till the soil." But later:

> And gentle Eve, the plaything of the gods,
> Erewhile a child, erewhile heat-lightning,
> Is now for him a young tigress,
> In the ominous glimmer of her pearls
> She is the herald of storm, and blood, and passion,
> And bitter joys, and somber misfortunes
> . . . .
>
> He struggles with her. Sly as a serpent,
> He enmeshes her in the nets of temptation.
> Here is Eve, the harlot, incoherently prattling,
> Here is Eve, the saint, with sorrowful eyes,
> Now a moon-maiden, now a maid of earth,
> But always and everywhere alien, alien.

The primary muse of Gumilev's *poemy* is the Muse of Distant
Travels; this is especially true of those written in the period
1910–12. The theme of travel, pilgrimage, adventure, discovery,
and of self-discovery through these activities, is central to "The
Northern Rajah," to the narrative cycle "The Return of Odysseus"
(I, 137–42), to the two *poemy* of *Foreign Skies,* "The Prodigal
Son" and "The Discovery of America," and also to the shorter
narrative "The Pilgrim" (I, 172–74), which is included in the
main body of *Skies* rather than in the *Poemy* section.

While not the central theme of "Adam's Dream," except in
the metaphorical sense that the poem portrays the spiritual
wanderings of mankind, it is an important subtheme.

"Otkrytie Ameriki" (The Discovery of America, I, 199–208; 285–87), first published in *Apollon* in 1910, is one of Gumilev's longest and most significant *poemy*. The Muse of Distant Travels is not only the poem's inspiration, she is one of its personae. She is mentioned several times by her full "title," and the whole poem is constructed as a dialogue between the poet and the Muse, both of whom accompany Columbus on his voyage. She serves as Columbus's muse as well as the poet's: "In the sound of the waves he hears a sweet summons, / The assurances of the Muse of Distant Travels" (I, 204).

Although the theme of the joy of travel and discovery themselves is reiterated several times in the poem, and although a good deal of the aesthetic pleasure the poem gives lies in the fine descriptions of the voyage and of the discovery of the New World, the real intent of the poem is not so much to describe and evoke the joys of travel, as to present travel and discovery as simply one manifestation, although a vivid one, of the "pathos of endeavor." The poem might be seen as a poetic illustration of Dostoevsky's comment that Columbus was happy, not when he had discovered America, but when he was in the process of discovering it. In Canto 3, when landfall has been made, Columbus does not rejoice, but grieves. His feat accomplished, he feels empty and useless:

> The tough wine-skin is proud of the wine it holds,
> But when no wine is left in it,
> Let its owner discard the wretched lump!
> I am a shell without a pearl,
> I am a stream that was dammed,
> But now released, I serve no purpose.   (I, 208)

The voyage completed, the Muse is no longer Columbus's, but the poet's alone: "The Muse of Distant Travels has abandoned him, / Like a lover, for other pastimes . . . As though in a dream, I heard my companion / Whisper to me, 'Grieve not for him / Who is called Columbus . . . Let us leave!' " The poem is not entirely a dialogue between the poet and the Muse: while the poet repeatedly addresses the Muse, she speaks only in these last lines.

In "Bludnyi syn" (The Prodigal Son, I, 196–99), written in amphibrachic tetrameter quatrains, Gumilev reinterprets the biblical tale as the story of the downfall of one who is false to the pathos of endeavor. It is that pathos which induces the son to leave his father's house:

> But you see, father, I yearn for something else,
> Yes, this world holds tears, but it also holds struggles.
>
> Was it for this, father, that I was born and grew up,
> Handsome, strong, and brimming with health,
> For the choir of your church to take the place of the
>   joy of victories
> . . . .
>
> You weep over sinners, but I am indignant,
> With the sword will I implant freedom and brotherhood,
> With fire will I teach love to the brutish.

But once out in the world the youth yields to its temptations, changes his values, and becomes a Roman hedonist: "I was sent here to reform vices. / But in a world ruled by falsity, / Having fathomed the doctrines of Roman philosophers, / I see only one vice—slovenliness, / And one virtue—elegant boredom." Thenceforth his fate is the same as that of the biblical youth: he becomes a slave, repents having left home, returns, and is received with joy and forgiveness. The moral of the biblical tale, though, is at odds with Gumilev's presumed intent, and his retention of the "happy ending" as in the Bible is inconsistent with his reinterpretation of the biblical story in terms of the pathos of endeavor, since at the end the youth not only has renounced his dissolute life in Rome, but also, by implication, has accepted his father's values of submissive piety and humble family life, the same values he had rejected upon setting out into the world.

The inspiration of the Muse of Distant Travels and the pathos of endeavor is also present in Gumilev's next two pieces of narrative poetry, "Iambic Pentameters" and *Mik*. Since I have already discussed the former in Chapter Four, I will only add that in this poem Gumilev finds an outlet for the pathos of endeavor not in travel, which is presented as a part of his past, but in war and in a religious calling.

With 1,031 lines, *Mik* (II, 205–38) is Gumilev's longest *poema* by a wide margin: the second longest, "The Discovery of America," has 252 lines, 336 including Canto Four. Although first published in full only in 1918, in a separate edition,[2] with the subtitle "An African Poem," the poem was written no later than 1913, since Gumilev read it at a meeting of the Society of Adepts of the Artistic Word at the beginning of 1914. It was then apparently not in its final form, as a note in *Apollon* reporting the reading speaks of it as having 960 lines.[3] It is written in unstanzaed iambic tetrameters and is divided into ten numbered sections, ranging in length from 75 to 142 lines and in turn divided into verse paragraphs of varying length. All rhymes are masculine, and most of the lines are rhymed as couplets.

The argument of the poem is as follows. The title character, a Negro slave-boy taken in battle by an Abyssinian warrior, is befriended by Louis, the ten-year-old son of the French consul in Addis Ababa. The two boys decide to run away, together with Mik's only other friend, an old captive baboon, to the city of the apes. Louis becomes king of the apes, but soon grows bored, and goes off alone into the jungle, where he hopes to become king of a more noble animal, the panthers. He is killed by the panthers, and Mik makes a journey to the underworld in search of his friend, but learns that he is in Heaven (since he is a Christian), and sends a skylark "beyond the stars" to bring him news of Louis. The story line then takes a jump, and Mik, now alone, helps a white ivory-hunter find the burial ground of the elephants, is enriched by the ivory, and becomes a great lord in Addis Ababa and an advisor to the Negus Menelik.

With its plot element of a young boy living among the jungle animals and communicating with them in their own tongue, the work is somewhat reminiscent of the Mowgli stories in Rudyard Kipling's *The Jungle Book*. And Gumilev's choice of a name for his boy-hero might well be an oblique acknowledgment of influence: Mik spelled backwards gives Kim.

The poem is a strange combination of playfulness and serious-

ness. As the résumé indicates, in plot terms it is a child's ad-
venture tale (at one point, Louis wishes that his adventures
could be described in the popular science magazine *Vokrug sveta*
[Around the World] by his favorite adventure writer, Louis
Boussenard), and according to Gumilev's sister-in-law, his son
Lev could recite it by heart at the age of eight.[4]

On the other hand, the report of the 1914 reading of the
poem indicates that the author considered it a serious piece of
literature. Aside from the very fact that he presented it to such
an august forum as the Society of Adepts of the Artistic Word,
Gumilev made the reading an occasion for an exposition of
"his views on the epic genre . . . and its contemporary poten-
tialities. His basic idea amounted to a claim that the only sphere
in which significant epic poetry (*bol'shoe epicheskoe tvorchestvo*)
is still possible is that of exotic poetry."[5] His remarks were followed by discussion, and again, if we can judge by the contemporary report, the participants took Gumilev's poem and his
views seriously.

In any case, however Gumilev and his colleagues may have
viewed the work, the text itself presents a mixture of playful
and serious elements. Some of the boys' adventures are purely
humorous. For example, they meet with the caravan of a wealthy
merchant's daughter, who invites Louis to come live with her
in her palace. His contemptuous refusal sounds like the reaction
of preadolescent boys anywhere to the company of girls:

> "I'd be bored with you:
> You can't shoot a gun,
> You're afraid to ride a horse."
>
> The princess stared at proud Louis
> With a long, meek, sad
> Gaze—and suddenly,
> Suddenly burst into laughter . . . And all around
> Began to laugh. It was as if thunder
> Resounded in the night air:
> After all, all five hundred
> Huge negros, eight hundred slaves,
> And thirty cooks, and nineteen
> Grooms were laughing.   (II, 220)

Besides humorous scenes such as this, there are smaller touches of humor. For example, when the city of the apes is described as a towering cliff, its face riddled with hundreds of round holes interconnected by a narrow path and each with its little clay ledge "like balconies," the narrator remarks in one of his rare personal comments: "I . . . would go so far as to say / That it was for all the world/Like an American skyscraper" (II, 221–22).

On the other hand, there are in the boys' adventure—once we have made the necessary suspension of disbelief—elements of tragedy (Louis's death) and of high seriousness (Mik's courageous and touching devotion to his friend in risking his life to save Louis from the panthers and to look for him in Hades). Gumilev's main intent in writing *Mik* may have been to entertain children, but the poem does express some of his seriously held beliefs. The "pathos of endeavor" is an important element in the poem: Louis refuses to be content with ruling such a peaceful "people" as the apes and boldly goes alone among the panthers; Mik braves any dangers and obstacles to see his friend once more. One of the major themes is the relationship between white civilization and the indigenous tribes of Africa. When Mik tells his friend the baboon of Louis's desire to become the king of the apes, the baboon is skeptical:

> He sensed, in his beast's heart,
> That there is a law in the world
> That gives to each of us
> Just one kind of experience:
> To some—life amidst urban pleasures,
> To others—the smell of wilderness grasses.
>
> . . . .
>
> And he muttered, taking a drink of water:
> "Look out that it doesn't come to ill!"   (II, 215)

And in fact Louis, the representative, as Strakhovsky says, of white supremacy,[6] at first assumes a position of sovereignty by virtue of sheer audacity and self-confidence, but remains alien and isolated, and perishes because he fails to understand the laws of the wild. On the other hand, the native Mik, closely allied with both the natural and the supernatural (the Forest Spirit) forces of the jungle, survives and prospers.

The mixture of playfulness and seriousness extends also to the diction of the poem. There is a good deal of highly colloquial speech interspersed throughout the poem; e.g., " 'OK, OK,' quailed the fraud, / 'Go on, go on, I didn't mean nothin' " (*Nu, nu,—otvetil, strusiv, plut,— / Idite s Bogom, chto uzh tut*) or "Why should you hang around here?" (*Tebe zdes' nechego torchat'*). But as soon as the narrative grows more serious, the diction becomes formal, elevated, "poetic": "Though there was only night on all sides, / Yes, only night, black as pitch, / And terror, and the wild water. / And in the moans of the wounded beast, / A pain that never dies" (II, 224–25); "Where the palm trees wave / Their fans at the grey clouds, / Where the velvet carpet of the meadows / Burns, all scarlet with flowers, / And where a spring ripples and rings, / Sad Mik buried Louis" (II, 227–28); "There it fell to the skylark / To see such glory, / That his feeble heart / Burst from joy" (II, 234).

After *Mik*, Gumilev's production of narrative poetry declines. Other than *Mik*, and "Iambic Pentameters," there are no narrative pieces in the period 1913–18. But between 1918 and 1921 he wrote two complete *poemy*, "Sentimental Journey" and "Stellar Terror," and worked on two others that he left uncompleted ("Two Dreams" and "Poem of the Beginning"). These later *poemy* manifest a change of direction analogous to developments in Gumilev's lyric poetry. The pathos of endeavor and the Muse of Distant Travels no longer hold the position they did in the earlier *poemy*, while motifs of mysticism and religion, prominent in the *poemy* of *Path of Conquistadors* but of lesser importance in the following *poemy*, here return to the fore.

"Sentimental'noe puteshestvie" (Sentimental Journey, II, 179–82) is the exception to the generalizations just made. Written in 1920 in three-stress *dol'niks*, rhymed abab but not divided into stanzas, and not published in Gumilev's lifetime, this poem describes an imagined voyage made by the poet and his beloved through the Bosporus to Athens and on to Port Said. The narration is in the present tense, and only toward the end do we discover that the whole voyage has been a dream:

> I recall, that in the past there was
> A moon, black as black Hades,
> We parted, and only with verses
> Could I try to entice you back.
> And as soon as I recall—the slender palms
> Disappear, and the fountain stops gushing;
> A big ship no longer awaits us
> To travel on, further south.
> It's an evil Petersburg night;
> I'm alone, my pen in my hand,
> And no one can help
> My inconsolable anguish.   (II, 181–82)

In his anguish, the poet is even uncertain whether it is the voyage that is the dream, or the "evil Petersburg night": "I have no more strength, I know not / Which is the dream. Are you cruel, / Or tender, and mine?" The woman to whom the poem is addressed might be any of a number of Gumilev's loves, or perhaps there is no concrete addressee. However, the tone of retrospection, certain specific phrases—such as "I love, I love undyingly / All that sang in your words"—and a subtle similarity of emotional texture between this poem and earlier lyrics addressed to Akhmatova, seem to indicate that "Sentimental Journey" is Gumilev's last poetic reminiscence of his love for her.

"Sentimental Journey" obviously belongs to the lyro-epic mode. "Stellar Terror" and "Poem of the Beginning"[7] are strictly in the narrative mode, with no element of the poet's personal emotional life; in fact they have very little in common with Gumilev's other *poemy* other than a distant affinity with those of *Path of Conquistadors*. Although very different in subject matter from one another, they belong to the same genre: they are the late Gumilev's attempts at mythopoeic poetry.

"Zvezdnyi uzhas" (Stellar Terror, II, 62–68)[8] is the closing poem of *Pillar of Fire*. There is no evidence available as to exactly when it was written. It consists of 195 lines of unrhymed and unstanzaed trochaic pentameter. The ostensible subject is primitive man's discovery of the stars. The setting is the prehistoric Near East; the personae, a tribe of nomadic herders. When the poem opens, the tribe's patriarch has just, first of his people, seen the night sky: he had gone to sleep "as one should," with his face to the ground, rolled over in a dream and waked up with his face to the sky. The sight has struck terror in his heart: "Woe! Woe! Fear, the noose and the pit / For him who is born on the earth,[9] / For the black one gazes on him / From the sky with so many eyes / And spies out his secrets." His eldest son, Gar, is curious to see "who it is who wanders in the sky," looks up, and is struck dead on the spot. Next, Gar's wife dares to look, but out of a desire for vengeance rather than out of curiosity: "I want to see his face, / Slash his throat with my teeth / And claw out his eyes with my nails"—and the sight drives her mad. The terrified tribe decides that the sky-dweller must want a sacrifice, and chooses an unstained girl-child, Gar's daughter. They place her face up on a stone and wait for her to die, but she, looking at the stars with a child's innocence and lack of preconceptions, sees there not terror, but beauty and knowledge:

> "I see nothing. Only the sky,
> Curved, black, empty,
> And in the sky, lights everywhere,
> Like flowers in a swamp in the spring."
>
> . . . .
>
> "No," she said, "they're not flowers,
> They are only golden fingers
> That point out to us the plain
> And the sea and the mountains of the Zends,
> And show us what has happened,
> What is happening and what will happen."   (II, 67)

Then she begins to sing, and one by one the whole tribe follows suit: they lie down with their faces to the sky and sing. Only the old man goes off alone to mourn the former times, when people looked

> At the plain where their herds grazed,
> At the water where their sails ran,
> At the grass where their children played,
> But not at the black sky, where glisten
> The inaccessible, alien stars.   (II, 68)

Thus the ostensible subject is man's discovery of the stars, but the real subject is his discovery of the world around him, as it is and as his physical senses, aesthetic sense, and intellect interpret it to him, and not as tradition, fear, and ignorance present it. It is not accidental that Gumilev chose the stars as the vehicle for this message. Star imagery is important throughout Gumilev's poetry, from the first poem in his first collection to the final poem in his last. Very often the image of a star represents some ideal to be striven for. In his Acmeist manifesto, in censuring Symbolism's attempts to comprehend the sphere of the unknown, he used the stars as a symbol of that sphere: "All the beauty, all the sacred significance of the stars lies in the fact that they are infinitely distant from the earth, and no successes of aviation will bring them closer" (IV, 174). And Nadezhda Mandelstam quotes him as having said that the stars have a different meaning for every poet.[10]

"Poema nachala" (Poem of the Beginning, II, 239–47), had it been completed as planned, apparently would have been Gumilev's most substantial narrative poem. The extant part was published in 1921, before his death, in the first issue of the miscellany of the postwar Poets' Guild. It was then reprinted in the second edition of his *Posthumous Poetry*[11] with a note indicating that it was written in 1918–19, and that twelve parts were planned. This part carries the subtitle "Book One: The Dragon"—so that the poem is often referred to by the title "The Dragon" and a subheading, "Canto One." Presumably the twelve planned parts referred to in the note would have been twelve cantos, which would have been grouped into more than one "Book." In any case, the completed Canto One consists of twelve numbered sections of twenty lines each. The meter is a three-stress *dol'nik* (this is Gumilev's longest work in *dol'niks*) rhymed AbAb, but not divided into stanzas.

In accord with the poem's projected massive scope, the mythopoeic ambitions of "Poem of the Beginning" are much greater than those of "Stellar Terror." It is, or aims at being, no less than an original, invented cosmology-mythology.

The dragon of the title is an ancient divinity, "the sovereign of ancient races." It has just awakened, after a sleep of ten centuries, to its last day of life on earth. The priest Moradita, a man taller and stronger than the trees, knowing this, has come to the dragon to persuade it, before it dies, to impart to man its knowledge "Of the origin, the transmutation / And the terrible end of the worlds." The two do not use speech; they communicate by their gaze, and by symbols, which the man draws in the sand, and the dragon forms by the play of light and color on its scales. The dragon answers contemptuously:

> "Are there, then, no more of the mighty,
> That I should give you my knowledge?
> I will entrust it to a scarlet rose,
> To the waterfalls and the clouds;
> I will entrust it to mountain ridges,
> The custodians of inert being,
>
> . . . .
>
> But not to a warm-blooded creature
> That doesn't know how to glitter!"   (II, 244)

Moradita is angered by the reply, refuses to accept the loss of the dragon's knowledge to man, and dares to speak aloud the forbidden word: Om. The sound of the forbidden word convulses the universe, and the shaken dragon tries to escape in death from the force of the man's will. Moradita understands what is happening, and pulls the dragon's foot to himself so that its claws will lacerate his breast. The blood from the wound flows over the dragon's scales, infusing it with life. The dragon rises into the air, and when Moradita repeats with his gaze his question

> About the birth, the transmutation
> And the end of the primal forces,
> The scales' coruscations illumined
> Far around the ledges of the cliffs,
> Like an inhuman voice
> Transformed from sound into light.   (II, 247)

The Canto ends here, but the apparent implication is that the coruscations of the dragon's scales conveyed the knowledge the priest was seeking. The content of the message, and its effect on mankind, would presumably have been the subject of succeeding cantos.

Moradita's quest represents man's attempt to establish contact with higher spheres of existence, with the divine, and through that contact to gain teleological knowledge. Man's main allies in this quest for knowledge are the power of the word—undoubtedly to be understood as the artistic word, the poetic word—and the force of his own will. Moradita first communicates with the dragon by symbol because he "did not want to reveal / To the beast the wondrous secret of words" (II, 243), but when it becomes necessary, he resorts to the secret word Om, to the "hitherto unknown power of the word" (II, 245–46). But it is his strength of will that gives him the courage to use the word. When the dragon answers with its refusal to impart its knowledge,

> Human strength resisted
> An intolerable fate,
>
> . . . .
>
> His lips opened, and . . .
>
> . . . .
>
> For the first time human lips
> Dared to speak it in the light of day,
> For the first time since the beginning of time
> Resounded the forbidden word: Om! (II, 244–45)

And again, when the dragon attempts to resist even the power of that word, when it seems that "he will escape from the human will / That burns his heart," the man finds the courage to sacrifice his own blood to gain the knowledge he seeks. His will refuses to recognize an impassable barrier between himself and the gods, and is determined to overcome any obstacles to his quest, even the resistance of the gods themselves. If in one of his first long poems Gumilev exclaimed "We will wrest the truth from God / With the force of flaming swords" ("Tale of the Kings"), then in this, one of his last, he gives that image a more explicit content: man will wrest the truth from the gods with the force of the word and of an unbendable will.

II *Dramatic Poetry*

Gumilev left a small but rather interesting body of dramatic poetry, consisting of six works of widely varying size, scope, style, and subject matter. They fall into two groups: three short, one-act plays, written in 1911–13, and three longer works, written in 1916–18.

Although the plays are very different from one another in tone and style as well as in setting and subject matter, they are all very closely related to one another, and to Gumilev's lyric poetry, in terms of underlying theme, of major character types and their problematics. In all six plays, the main hero— a poet, either literally or figuratively—is juxtaposed to one or more other male characters who represent in one form or another the "antipoetic" principle. In some cases, these antagonists seem to represent the Philistinism of the outer world, the pragmatic, the unimaginative, or pedestrian. In other cases they seem to represent rather an exteriorization of the worldliness within the poet's own personality, the sensuality that weighs him down in his search for the ideal. Thus it might be said that in his body of dramatic works Gumilev shows the poet in conflict with the world and with himself. In the three early plays (*Don Juan in Egypt, Actaeon, The Card Game*),[12] the emphasis is on the conflict with the outer world; in the later plays (*Gondla, The Child of Allah, The Poisoned Tunic*), the poet-pragmatist conflict is present, but is subordinated to the conflict between the sensualist and the idealist, which is basically a projection of the inner psychological conflict that Gumilev felt between opposing facets of his own complex character.[13] The most complex and interesting of the plays are those in which the dramatic conflict is most closely intertwined with the author's inner conflict: *Gondla* and *The Poisoned Tunic*.

The three early plays, while similar in problematics, are quite different from one another in other respects. *Don Juan in Egypt* is a humorous fantasy with occasional serious notes. The verse is fluent but undistinguished. The other two are cast in a serious vein. The "realistic" setting of *The Card Game* (a gaming house in Paris in 1813) is rather inappropriate to the highly exalted diction of the play, which is clearly the weakest of the six; the verse is often clumsy, the imagery bathetic. *Actaeon*, an adaptation of the Greek myth to Gumilev's purposes, is the most successful of the early plays. The verse maintains a higher and more consistent standard of excellence; particularly impressive is the skill with which Gumilev varies the meter—and correspondingly the diction—to accord with the characters of the various personae. Furthermore, the play's theme is more serious than that of *Don Juan* and more skillfully worked out than that of *The Card Game*. Actaeon embodies the tragic fate of the poet, caught between two levels of existence. Conscious of his superiority to ordinary mortals, as shown in his conflict with the pragmatic Cadmus, he aspires to rise to the level of the gods, and is punished for his presumption.

The Child of Allah, first published in 1917, contrasts to the other two late plays in its light, humorous, even (in the outcome) joyous tone, a tone which reflects its origin. Subtitled "An Arabian Fairy-Tale in Three Scenes," it was written for a marionette theater organized by some members of the *Apollon* group under the inspiration of the English actor and director Gordon Craig's marionette version of *Hamlet*.[14] Both the language and the characters are highly stylized, in a manner appropriate to a puppet theater and using the stylistic and legendary material of the Near Eastern poetic tradition. The heroine is a peri, and the hero Hafiz is supposedly the fourteenth-century Persian poet of that name, so that despite the subtitle, the play draws at least as much on the Persian tradition as on the Arabic.

But although the play lacks all solemnity and pathos, there are serious themes underlying the glitter of the play's stylistic surface. The joyous outcome of the third act is a harmonious resolution of scenes of death, human baseness, pangs of conscience, and a search for atonement in the first two acts, which, however, due to the stylization and the humorous treatment, do not create the somber colors and mood of analogous scenes in *Gondla*. Like the other plays, though in a very different key, *The Child of Allah* is concerned with the nature and role of the poet, and his relationships to other men, to women, to the external world, and to the world of the spirit. The ideal figure of the poet is embodied in the play's hero, Hafiz, a representative of, in Vsevolod Sechkarev's felicitous phrase, "joyous wisdom" (III, xvii). His is a balanced wisdom, which knows both the world of the spirit and the pleasures of the physical world, the beauties of art, nature, and love. He is contrasted both to characters who embody positive traits, but are one-sided (such as the Bedouin, a fearless warrior), and to characters who embody nothing but base traits.

Gondla, subtitled "A Dramatic Poem in Four Acts," was first published in the first issue of the journal *Russkaya mysl* for 1917, and thus probably written in 1916. The setting is Iceland in the ninth century, and the central conflict is between the crude, pagan, and barbarous Icelandic mores, and the ideals of Christianity and of art, represented by the Irish and primarily by the title hero Gondla, a lutenist and singer. This conflict in turn may be seen as a representation of the inner conflict that Gumilev felt between the two sides of his own character: the warrior—the earthly, sensuously passionate, straightforwardly courageous man of action, self-confident and proficient in "manly" activities such as hunting, war, carousing, and seduction—versus the poet—the mild, shy, tender, devoutly religious idealist, for whom love is a pure, spiritual experience and a doorway to the sphere of the ideal.

This is the first of Gumilev's plays that as a piece of poetry can stand comparison with his better lyrical and narrative poetry. The lyricism and the deep religious feeling of Gondla's speeches are poetically fine and convincing, and while his speeches are of course the high points of the play, the quality of the verse is sustained on a high level virtually throughout, with only a few weak lines or passages. In contrast to the iambs that Gumilev uses in all the other plays, except for parts of *Actaeon,* *Gondla* is written entirely in anapestic trimeter, rhymed AbAb.

Gumilev's last play, *Otravlennaia tunika* (The Poisoned Tunic, III, 137–210; 179–227), was not published in his lifetime. He wrote most if not all of it in 1917–18, in Paris and London.

Gumilev drew on Byzantine history for the setting of his play, some of the characters, and several important plot elements, but it is not a historical play in that it is not primarily concerned with historical accuracy, and, as Professor Struve points out, "is not built around historical events, but around a personal conflict and a personal problem."[15] The play takes place in the court of Justinian. The emperor and his empress, Theodora, play important roles in the central love-intrigue, but are not among the principals. Of the principals in the love triangle, only one is based on a historical figure: the character of the poet Imr is based closely on what is known of the life and poetry of the sixth-century Arab poet Imru'-al-Qays, and on the legends connected with him. The heroine, Zoe, Justinian's daughter, is pure invention, and the third member, the King of Trebizond, has no connection with any specific historical person (in the sixth century, Trebizond was part of the Byzantine Empire and had no king), and indeed is not even given a name in the play. The only other character, the Eunuch, is a historical type rather than a historical figure.

With five acts and nearly 1,500 lines, *The Poisoned Tunic* is Gumilev's longest, most significant, and most successful play, the only one that is truly a dramatic work in every sense of the word. Gumilev himself was undoubtedly fully conscious of this: note his subtitle, "A tragedy," versus "A dramatic poem" (*Gondla*) and "An Arabian fairy-tale" (*The Child of Allah*). In form and structure, Gumilev closely followed all the rules of neo-Classical tragedy. He observes the unities of time, place (the whole play takes place in one room, in the imperial palace in Constantinople, in the space of twenty-four hours—although a night passes between the third and fourth acts), and action. To the three unities is added what Pushkin called the fourth unity: unity of style. The entire play is sustained on the elevated level of style appropriate to tragedy. At the same time, within this unified "high" style, Gumilev skillfully varies the style of speech of the several characters, giving each a style appropriate to his position and personality. For example, Imr's style is passionate, energetic, full of poetic, sometimes extravagant, imagery; Justinian's is judicious, restrained, pragmatic; the King of Trebizond's is forthright, simple, dignified. The main characters are of noble rank, and the number of characters is limited to those absolutely necessary to the plot. In most of the scenes, only two people are on stage, and in only one are there

more than three. The verse form is not the Alexandrine of French
Classical tragedy, but the blank verse of Elizabethan tragedy.
Also as in Shakespearean blank verse, there are occasional rhymed
passages, but here they occur in the speeches of only one of the
characters: Imr the poet speaks most of the time in rhyme, although some of his speeches are also unrhymed.

The plot is a rather complex one of Byzantine intrigue, which
must be summarized here in highly simplified form. When the
play opens, Imr has just arrived in Constantinople to ask the
emperor's aid in reconquering his late father's small kingdom
in Arabia. He sees Zoe in the palace and falls in love with
her before he knows who she is. Justinian has just betrothed
Zoe to the King of Trebizond, for political purposes: he plans
to murder the king immediately after the wedding, by means of
a poisoned bridal tunic, in order to annex Trebizond to the
empire. Theodora, meanwhile, sees in Imr's passion for Zoe an
opportunity to take revenge on her stepdaughter (Gumilev's
invention: Justinian had only one wife, Theodora, and no children), who once insulted her. She maneuvers the two into a
rendezvous. When the king learns of this, he commits suicide;
when Justinian learns of it, he orders that Imr be killed, by
the poisoned tunic, and that Zoe be confined in a convent the
rest of her life.

The play is complex not only in plot. It has several levels
of meaning, including possibly a topical political subtext. But it is
above all a tragedy of the fragility of love in a world dominated
by evil. The play's outcome is the complete triumph of evil,
as embodied in Theodora. Justinian is punished by the loss
of his daughter and heir for his plot to use immoral means to his
imperial aims, and Imr, the king, and Zoe, none of whom com-
mitted any worse sin than to love "not wisely, but too well,"
are all destroyed utterly, the two men physically, and Zoe
morally. Of the three, it might be said that Imr is the most
culpable. The most passionate of the three, he allowed the
strength of his passions to draw him into the Byzantine atmosphere of intrigue; he tried to use Theodora's weapons against
her, but as a simple Arab, an essentially honest and upright poet
and warrior, he naturally came off second best in the contest
with the native Byzantine, Theodora.

The primary link between *The Poisoned Tunic* and Gumilev's other plays lies in the role of the hero Imr as poet. While only four of Gumilev's six dramatic heroes are literally poets or singers (Actaeon, Gondla, Hafiz, and Imr), they are all in some sense subjective, projections of one or more facets of his own character. The inner conflict that he felt between his "poet-self"—the idealist who finds links with the ideal in his poetry and in love—and his "warrior-self"—the man of action and earthly passion—is projected in various ways in the several plays. Of all the plays, in *The Poisoned Tunic* the situation is the most complex, for here, while the poet-hero Imr is opposed to the warrior-hero, he himself is also a warrior and a man of passion. In fact, there is little of the idealist in Imr, and the love that he sought so energetically, when it comes, does not elevate him to the sphere of the ideal, but brings with it pain and shame:

> The whole night passed in strange and wondrous visions,
> The whole night long, my soul was on the rack.
> An eagle soared in unknown heights,
> And its scream was like the clash of steel swords.
> But often, through the crash of steel
> Broke a piercing, inconsolable lament,
> And some unknown lightning flashed . . .
> There was a dark shame, inevitable as death,
> More bitterly dispiriting than death . . .
> At the heels of this woman, so beloved,
> Shame slunk along dark lanes.   (III, 182)

The king is physically stronger than Imr, and, it is implied, is his superior as a warrior; but he is only a warrior; like his counterparts in *The Child of Allah*, he is one-sided. A man of absolute honesty and forthrightness, he is morally a more admirable character than Imr, and his fate more pitiable. Imr still is the more attractive, for he has what the king lacks—inspiration and passion, those two inalienable qualities of the true poet. Yet Imr, though a true poet, is not the ideal poet. His passions are diverted only "outward," not "upward," and thus he too must perish, perish pointlessly at what appears to be his moment of triumph, and his death does not bring about a victory of the principle of good, as does Gondla's. It is certainly no mere coincidence, but one further indication of the subjective inspiration of Gumilev's plays, that *Gondla* and *The Child of Allah*, written in 1916, when Gumilev had just recently proven his physical and spiritual mettle on the field of combat, end on notes of optimism; while *The Poisoned Tunic*, written in 1917–18, when Russia's situation and prospects must have appeared grim to the patriot and monarchist Gumilev and when his own emotional life was in upheaval, ends on a note of black pessimism.

CHAPTER 6

Conclusion

GUMILEV'S highly visible role as founder and leader of Acmeism, a school nominally opposed to Symbolism and designated variously as neo-Parnassian, neo-Classical, and neo-Realistic, has tended to confuse the issue of his relationship as a poet to Symbolism, and to obscure to some degree the central importance of the Romantic outlook in his life and art. Yury Verkhovsky ends his analysis of Gumilev's development with the conclusion that the mature Gumilev's poetic art was, after all, symbolistic, and other critics have spoken of a "return to Symbolism." I do not propose in this brief concluding chapter to investigate the complicated question of Gumilev's changing and contradictory relationships to the Symbolist School. In any case, this sort of classification, while it may serve to provide a point of departure for analysis, tells us but little about the inner essence of an individual artist. I raise the question here only because I believe that if the "Acmeist" Gumilev did indeed owe a continuing debt to that child of Romanticism, Symbolism, this is only one manifestation—and probably not the most significant one—of the fact that throughout his creative life he remained a Romantic idealist, with all that that implies for his art, in terms of themes and their treatment.

Gumilev's Romantic idealism found its expression primarily in two areas, love and the "pathos of endeavor." Both areas must be taken into account for a full and proper understanding of the poet, and one of my aims in this book has been to move toward a more balanced perception of his work by indicating the considerable significance of the love theme, alongside the themes of travel and adventure. Just as the public image of Gumilev the Acmeist *maître* has tended to obscure his ties with Symbolism, so the public image of Gumilev the poet-warrior

171

has tended to obscure his other face, that of Gumilev the tender lyricist.

As Gumilev developed and matured, and freed himself from external influences, the strain of personal lyricism in his poetry freed itself from the restraints imposed on it by his adopted "macho" pose, and won its way to a more direct and open expression in his later poetry. But the theme of love is a powerful presence in his poetry from the beginning, and while there are sharp differences between his early and late work in the stylistic expression of that theme, there are also clear links in the philosophical treatment. Although the expression of the theme became more "realistic," i.e., more concretely personal in the later poetry, Gumilev never abandoned his Romantic ideal of love, his search in life and in poetry for the Ideal Woman, a love and a woman capable of transfiguring earthly reality, of lifting the lovers onto another, higher level of existence.

The "pathos of endeavor" in Gumilev has two major aspects: that of physical endeavor, and that of spiritual endeavor. Again, the image of Gumilev the poet-warrior has tended to emphasize the importance of the former at the expense of the latter. The pathos of physical endeavor—adventure, travel, exploration, combat, and the like—is certainly one primary element of Gumilev's life and art. But no less significant, and a more organic manifestation of his Romantic idealism, is the pathos of spiritual endeavor—the striving for spiritual and cultural achievement, the drive to form of one's life-activity a significant and lasting legacy to the treasure-house of the human spirit. The latter, in fact, underlies and gives rise to the former. Columbus, for example, earns the poet's admiration, not for his pragmatic contribution of opening the way to the New World, but because his whole enterprise was an expression of the spiritual qualities of unbending will and unflinching courage.

For Gumilev, the primary arena for the manifestation of the pathos of spiritual endeavor was of course art, and specifically poetry. He shared the Romantics' view of the poet as a superior being, and was wholly convinced that, since he had been endowed with the gift—or the curse—of an artist's soul, he had no choice but to devote the full force of his spirit, will, and talent always and in all things to surpass the ordinary human being, to be a leader and a guide to humanity on the path to the Ideal.

Whatever the place in Russian literature the ongoing critical evaluation and scholarly investigation of Russian Modernism may eventually afford him, and whatever his human shortcomings, Gumilev should always stand as an example of the totally dedicated artist-idealist. In the end, however, an artist must be evaluated not on the basis of intent, however exalted and energetically pursued, but on achievement. On this score, Gumilev's *oeuvre* need not fear a closer critical examination. A poet of considerable if somewhat uneven talent, who developed slowly, almost painfully, but steadily, who never entirely overcame the aesthetic deficiencies so apparent in his earliest poetry, but who nonetheless throughout his career exhibited a gradually growing intensity of feeling and profundity of thought, imagination, and human insight, as well as a constantly increasing control of his craft, Nikolay Gumilev left as his legacy to Russian and world literature a remarkable body of poetry, a body which includes, to be sure, some weak or failed efforts, but also some of the finest achievements of twentieth-century Russian poetry. That body has earned him a permanent place in the pantheon of Russian poets. One of the tasks now before Russian literary scholarship is to clarify the extent and nature of the considerable influence that the poetry has had on other Russian poets, both in emigration and in the Soviet Union.

Notes and References

Chapter One

1. A. Gumileva, "Nikolai Stepanovich Gumilev," *Novyi zhurnal,* kn. 46 (1956), 108.
2. B. P. Koz'min, *Pisateli sovremennoi epokhi. Biobibliograficheskii slovar' russkikh pisatelei XX veka,* I (Moscow, 1928). This reference work gives a brief biographical note on which later writers on Gumilev have relied heavily. It will be referred to a number of times in this book.
3. Irina Odoevtseva, *Na beregakh Nevy* (Washington, D. C., 1967), p. 85.
4. Unfortunately, these reports are not from firsthand witnesses of Gumilev's school years. One is from Nikolay Otsup, a protégé of Gumilev who met him only after the Revolution (see his memoir on Gumilev in his book *Sovremenniki* (Paris, 1961), p. 25; another is from A. A. Gumileva, Gumilev's brother's wife, who first met him in 1909 (see Gumileva, op cit., p. 111). Sergey Makovsky is representative of those who doubt the validity of such reports; see his "Nicolas Gumilëv (1886–1921). Un témoignage sur l'homme et sur le poète," *Cahiers du monde russe et soviétique,* III, 2 (1962), 179. I have made extensive use of A. A. Gumileva's and Makovsky's articles.
5. Anna Akhmatova, *Sochineniia* (Munich, 1965), I, 84.
6. Makovsky, p. 194.
7. A. Gumileva, p. 112.
8. Ibid., pp. 112–13.
9. Published in the Paris newspaper *Poslednie novosti,* Oct. 23 and 25, 1921, and quoted in SS II, 349–51. See also a quite different version of the incident in Odoevtseva, pp. 174–75.
10. Georgii Ivanov, "O Gumileve," *Sovremennye zapiski,* t. 47 (1931), 309.
11. Makovsky, p. 187.
12. Sergei Makovskii, "Cherubina de Gabriak," in *Portrety sovremennikov,* by Sergei Makovskii (New York, 1955), p. 357. Earlier in the same article (pp. 342–45), Makovsky describes the other circumstances surrounding the duel. For a description of the duel

175

itself, which he did not witness, he quotes from A. N. Tolstoy's memoir, which is also excerpted in SS II, 351–53. Makovsky's and Tolstoy's versions of the preliminaries differ in some details, including the distance (Tolstoy gives fifteen paces).

13. A. Gumileva, p. 110.

14. Vera Nevedomskaia, "Vospominaniia o Gumileve i Akhmatovoi, *Novyi zhurnal*, kn. 38 (1954), 182–90.

15. A. Gumileva, p. 117.

16. Lev Gumilev is an ethnohistorian working in Leningrad. For further information on him, see Sam Driver, *Anna Akhmatova* (New York, 1972), pp. 33–34.

17. See Makovsky, "Nicolas Gumilev . . . ," p. 204.

18. A. Gumileva, p. 113.

19. A. Gumileva, p. 117.

20. Makovsky, "Nicolas Gumilev . . . ," p. 203.

21. Ibid., p. 206.

22. Leonid Strakhovsky, *Craftsmen of the Word* (1949; rpt. Westport, Conn., 1969), p. 37.

23. See SS I, liii–liv.

24. A. Gumileva, p. 125.

25. Georgii Ivanov, op. cit., ˈp. 316.

26. Odoevtseva, p. 14.

27. Ibid., p. 95.

28. Gleb Struve, *Soviet Russian Literature, 1917–50* (Norman, Okla., 1951), p. 45.

29. Odoevtseva, pp. 142–43.

30. In his sharply polemical 1918 article "With Neither Deity nor Inspiration" ("Bez bozhestva, bez vdokhnoven'ia," a quotation from one of Pushkin's most famous poems), Blok, as it were, revived the Acmeist-Symbolist controversy. Some lines in Gumilev's poem "My Readers" (first published in 1921), which taken only in the context of Gumilev's poetic development have such an anachronistic ring, should undoubtedly be seen as a brusque reply to Blok's article. I refer to the lines "I don't offend them [my readers—E.S.] with neurasthenia, / Don't degrade them with soft sentiment, / Don't bore them with weighty allusions / To the contents of a hollow egg" (II, 61).

31. Odoevtseva, p. 191.

32. Quoted in Strakhovsky, p. 51, and in Gleb Struve, "N. S. Gumilev, Zhizn' i lichnost'," SS I, xli.

33. Evgenii Zamiatin, *Litsa* (New York, 1967), p. 93.

34. Nadezhda Mandelstam, *Hope Against Hope: A Memoir* (New York, 1970), pp. 109–10.

35. Georgy Ivanov quotes the letter thus in his article "O Gumileve" (op. cit., p. 321), but somewhat differently elsewhere: "Don't worry about me, I feel fine; I'm reading Homer and writing poetry" (preface to the second edition of *Foreign Skies* [Berlin, 1936], pp. 3–4).

36. Most forcefully by Bertram Wolfe in his *The Bridge and the Abyss* (New York, 1967), pp. 121–29.

37. Quoted in Strakhovsky, loc. cit., and Struve, loc. cit. Cf. Odoevtseva, pp. 430–32 and 436–38.

38. A. Gumileva, p. 109.

39. Iurii Verkhovskii, "Put' poeta. O poezii N. S. Gumileva," *Sovremennaia literatura* (Leningrad, 1925), p. 108.

40. Ol'ga Forsh, *Sumasshedshii korabl'* (Washington, D. C., 1964), p. 157. This work is a slightly fictionalized memoir of life in the House of Arts; the title, *The Mad Ship*, is her term for the House.

41. D. S. Mirskii, "Valerii Iakovlevich Briusov," *Sovremennye zapiski*, no. 22 (1924), p. 414.

42. *Russkaia literatura XX veka (Dorevoliutsionnyi period)*, ed. N. S. Trifonov (Moscow, 1962), pp. 434–39.

Chapter Two

1. V. Briusov, *Vesy*, 1905, No. 11, p. 68. Reprinted in his *Dalekie i blizkie* (Moscow, 1912), p. 143.

2. See Odoevtseva, pp. 71–72.

3. Verkhovsky, p. 93.

4. A biblical allusion; the immediate source, however, was probably Bely's *Vtoraia simfoniia* (Second Symphony), where the "woman clothed with the sun" of Rev. 12:1 is a recurrent image.

5. There were two separate editions of *Romantic Flowers*, 1908 and 1918. Gumilev labeled the latter the "third edition," because in the 1910 edition of *Pearls* he had included a section entitled "Romantic Flowers" that consisted of twenty poems from the 1908 collection, plus one new one. The last edition is considerably larger than the first; it was expanded by several poems not previously collected, and by poems transferred from *The Path of Conquistadors* and *Pearls*. It has forty-five poems, totaling a little over a thousand lines.

6. V. Briusov, *Vesy*, 1908, no. 3, p. 77. Reprinted in *Dalekie i blizkie*, p. 144.

7. Published in the newspaper *Rech'*, for December 15, 1908, over the signature I. A., and reprinted as part of Gleb Struve's

article "Innokentii Annenskii i Gumilev: Neizvestnaia stat'ia Annenskogo," *Novyi zhurnal*, kn. 78 (1965), 279–87. Professor Struve was the first to bring to light this review, which does not figure in any of the Gumilev bibliographies, and which had never previously been attributed to Annensky.

8. For example, that of Mikhail Kuzmin, whose decadent influence can be seen in the occasional use of death, disease, decay, and the like as material for dispassionately descriptive poetry—as in "Zaraza" (The Plague), whose accentual meter perhaps also was suggested by Kuzmin. There are a number of other poems in *Flowers* and *Pearls* with a touch of Kuzminian decadence, including one dedicated to him: "V biblioteke" (In the Library).

9. Viktor Gofman, *Russkaia mysl'*, 1908, No. 7, p. 144 (of the third pagination).

10. Renato Poggioli, *The Poets of Russia, 1890–1930* (Cambridge, Mass., 1960), p. 98.

11. Bryusov, loc. cit.

12. Verkhovsky, p. 95.

13. Cf. Annensky's review: "Why must 'Pausanius the Sailor' and 'The Emperor Caracalla' necessarily be historical pictures? It is enough for me if, in their nice rhymes, in their gorgeous words, in the cultivated caprice of their perceptions, they are ornamental, be it only in the Parisian, or even the boulevard style." Cf. also Verkhovsky, p. 95.

14. The title was supplied only in the 1918 edition of *Flowers*; in the 1908 edition, in *Pearls*, and earlier in the journal *Vesy* (1906), it was printed without title.

15. "The Choice" did not appear in the 1908 edition. It was first published in a periodical in 1909, then in *Pearls*, in the section "Black Pearl"; then transferred to *Flowers* in 1918. It is translated in Burton Raffel and Alla Burago, *Selected Works of Nikolai S. Gumilev* (Albany, 1972), p. 34. This is no. 1 in the SUNY Press series *Russian Literature in Translation*, edited by Sidney Monas. Future references to translations in this volume will be given in the text, as a page-number reference in conjunction with the volume-page reference to the original. (e.g., I, 55; 34.)

16. The second edition of *Pearls* (1918) was considerably shorter than the 1910 edition. The "Romantic Flowers" section was omitted, several other poems were transferred to the 1918 edition of *Romantic Flowers*, and several more discarded. Even with these cuts, the 1918 *Pearls* is still Gumilev's largest collection of poems. He made other changes in the new edition: it is no longer divided into sections,

and while the first third of the book is close in contents and order to "Black Pearl," the order of the rest is significantly changed.
    17. V. Briusov, *Russkaia mysl'*, 1910, no. 7, pp. 206–208. Reprinted in *Dalekie i blizkie*, pp. 145–47.
    18. V. Ivanov, *Apollon*, 1910, no. 7, pp. 38–41.
    19. "The Duel" was revised for the 1918 edition of *Pearls*, primarily by the deletion of four stanzas, including the one just quoted. The revision improved, but did not redeem, the poem.
    20. Verkhovsky, p. 97.
    21. The 1918 edition, as mentioned in note 16 above, dispenses with the division into sections; all the cycles and narratives are placed at the end of the book, in the order: "Beatrice," "The Return of Odysseus," "Captains," "Adam's Dream." "The Northern Rajah" was discarded in this edition, and "Neo-Romantic Fairy-Tale" was transferred to the 1918 edition of *Romantic Flowers*.
    22. Verkhovsky, p. 98.
    23. See *The Penguin Book of Russian Verse*, p. 71, for the poem and a literal translation.

Chapter Three

    1. Mikhail Kuzmin, "Pis'ma o russkoi poezii," *Apollon*, 1912, no. 2, p. 73.
    2. Nikolai Gumilev, "Nasledie simvolizma i Akmeizm," *Apollon*, 1913, no. 1, pp. 42–45. Reprinted in *Pis'ma o russkoi poezii*, ed. Georgii Ivanov (Petrograd, 1923), and in SS IV, 171–76. Translated in Raffel and Burago, pp. 245–48, and in *Nikolai Gumilev on Russian Poetry*, ed. and trans. David Lapeza (Ann Arbor, Mich., 1977), pp. 21–24.
    3. Sergei Gorodetskii, "Nekotorye techeniia v sovremennoi russkoi poezii," *Apollon*, 1913, no. 1, p. 46–50.
    4. Kuzmin, loc. cit.
    5. Also translated in *The Abinger Garland* (see Bibliography), p. 13.
    6. Translated in *The Abinger Garland*, p. 7, under the title "Night Was Drawing In."
    7. In this charming poem, the only one in *Skies* in a lighter vein (although its humor is overshadowed by a poignantly sad note), Gumilev imitates folk-poetry style to characterize his wife as a sorceress: "From the lair of the serpent, / From the city of Kiev, / I took not a wife, but a witch."
    8. Verkhovsky, p. 106. The phrase "beautiful clarity" is from the title of an article by Mikhail Kuzmin ("O prekrasnoi iasnosti,"

Apollon, no. 4, 1910, which in its attack on Symbolist poetics anticipated the Acmeist position.
9. Ibid., p. 108.

Chapter Four

1. *Dol'nik* is the term now in general use in Russian prosody for a particular type of non-syllabo-tonic verse. It is narrower in meaning than the term accentual, or tonic, verse. Whereas the term "accentual" refers to all verse in which the only metrical constant is the number of stresses per line, and the number of syllables between stressed syllables is totally unregulated, in *dol'niki* the interstress interval is normally either one or two syllables, e.g., "Ia segodnia opiat' uslyshal, / Kak tiazhelyi iakor' polzet": $- - \angle - - \angle - \angle - /$ $- - \angle - \angle - - \angle$. A leading investigator distinguishes three types of *dol'niki*, which he labels with the names of the poets most instrumental in introducing each type: the Esenin type, the Gumilev type, and the Tsvetaeva type. See M. L. Gasparov, "Russkii trekhudarnyi dol'nik XX v.," in *Teoriia stikha* (Leningrad, 1968), pp. 97–106; see also my article *"Dol'niks* in Gumilev's Poetry," in *Toward a Definition of Acmeism*, ed. Denis Mickiewicz, supplementary issue of *Russian Language Journal* (Spring 1975), pp. 21–41.
2. M. Tumpovskaia, " 'Kolchan' N. Gumileva," *Apollon*, 6–7 (1917), p. 58.
3. Verkhovsky, p. 117.
4. Gleb Struve, "Tvorcheskii put' Gumileva," SS II, xxi.
5. Of the eleven Italian poems Gumilev wrote in 1912, he included seven in *The Quiver*: "Venice," "Rome," "Pisa," "The Cathedral at Padua," "Genoa," "Bologna," and "Naples." The other four are "Villa Borghese," "On the Palatine," "Florence," and "Lake Trasimeno." "Rome," "Pisa," and "Genoa" were published in *Russkaya mysl*, 1912, no. 7; and "Venice," "Bologna," and "Florence" in *Giperborey*, no. 6 (1913).
6. Verkhovsky, pp. 120–21.
7. I have translated only the two most lyrical stanzas. Complete translations, which will give the reader a better idea of the relationship between the lyrical and the descriptive, may be found in Raffel and Burago, p. 70; and in Strakhovsky, pp. 32–33.
8. Also translated in both Raffel and Burago (p. 72) and Strakhovsky (p. 32).
9. Tumpovskaya, p. 60.
10. Translated in Markov and Sparks (see preface), pp. 237–39.
11. Cf. for example in the twelfth-century *Slovo o polku Igoreve*:

"On the Nemiga the spread sheaves are heads, the flails that thresh are of steel, lives are laid out on the threshing floor, souls are winnowed from bodies. Nemiga's gory banks are . . . sown with the bones of Russia's sons" (*The Song of Igor's Campaign,* translated by Vladimir Nabokov [New York, 1960], p. 62).

12. B. Eikhenbaum, "Novye stikhi N. Gumileva," *Russkaia mysl',* 1916, no. 2, p. 18.

13. Similarly in the ballad "The Vagabond" (*Skies*), there is nothing concretely Russian, but the colloquial style (*Ish'! / Nachitalsia driani raznoi, / Vot i govrish'"*) gives a Russian flavor that leads the reader to assume a Russian setting.

14. Translated in full in Strakhovsky, pp. 35–36. Strakhovsky quotes Vladimir Nabokov's opinion of the poem as "one of the most remarkable poems ever written."

15. Tumpovskaya, p. 63.

16. A second edition was published in Revel (Tallinn) in 1922, i.e., after Gumilev's death, but from a ms. prepared by the poet himself. Most of the poems were considerably revised from the first edition, and four new ones were added ("The Suez Canal," "Madagascar," "Zambezi," and "The Niger").

17. N. Gumilev, *Izbrannoe,* ed. N. Otsup (Paris, 1959).

18. Strakhovsky, p. 49.

19. Also translated (in part) in Strakhovsky, p. 50.

20. Also translated in Markov and Sparks, pp. 241–43.

21. Verkhovsky, p. 123.

22. Cf. "The Comrade" (*Pearls*); "Sonnet" (*Foreign Skies*); "Stockholm" and "Pre-Memory" (*The Pyre*); "Olga" and "The Streetcar Gone Astray" (*Pillar of Fire*).

23. Verkhovsky, p. 124.

24. Innokentii Oksenov, "Pis'ma o sovremennoi poezii," *Kniga i revoliutsiia,* no. 1 (13), 1921), p. 31. Quoted in Strakhovsky, p. 49.

25. Strakhovsky, p. 49.

26. Also translated in *The Abinger Garland,* p. 12.

27. Also translated in *The Abinger Garland,* p. 6.

28. Gumilev's Paris album, by the way, contains a variant of this poem ("The Lost Day," II, 166) in which the nightmare element is entirely absent. It is interesting that Gumilev chose to publish the more ominous of the two variants.

29. Also translated in *The Penguin Book of Russian Verse,* pp. 295–97.

30. Stribog was the ancient Slavic god of the wind.

31. Verkhovsky, p. 120.

32. Also translated in Markov and Sparks, pp. 239–41, and in *The Penguin Book of Russian Verse*, pp. 297–98.

33. Verkhovsky, p. 137.

34. Translated in *The Abinger Garland*, pp. 11–12.

35. Also translated in *Russian Literature Triquarterly*, no. 1 (1971), pp. 8–9, and in *The Abinger Garland*, pp. 8–9.

36. Odoevtseva, pp. 72, 74.

37. Cf. Revelations 4:7. The "new Jerusalem" of the stanza just preceding these two (stanza 12) is no doubt also an allusion to Revelations (ch. 21), although the wording is also reminiscent of Isaiah 62:1. Professor Struve has pointed out the similarity in wording of this stanza to Blake's lines, "I will not cease from Mental Fight, / Nor shall my sword sleep in my hand / Till we have built Jerusalem / In England's green and pleasant land" (SS, II, 292).

38. Also translated in *Russian Literature Triquarterly*, no. 1 (Fall 1971), pp. 12–13; in *The Penguin Book of Russian Verse*, pp. 300–303; in Strakhovsky, pp. 46–48; and in Markov and Sparks, pp. 249–53.

39. Odoevtseva, p. 422.

40. Ibid., p. 423.

41. Makovskii, *Na Parnase "Serebrianogo veka"* (Munich, 1962), p. 207.

42. Also translated in *The Abinger Garland*, pp. 14–15, and in Markov and Sparks, pp. 243–45.

43. Also translated in Markov and Sparks, pp. 245–47.

44. Also translated in *Russian Literature Triquarterly*, no. 1 (Fall 1971), p. 10; in *The Penguin Book of Russian Verse*, pp. 299–300; and in Markov and Sparks, pp. 247–49.

45. Verkhovsky, p. 131. Cf. also Dmitrii Klenovskii, "Okkul'tnye motivy v russkoi poezii nashego veka," *Grani*, 20 (1953), 129–37. Klenovsky quotes the above-cited passage from Gumilev's manifesto ("To keep in mind always the unknowable, but not offend one's thoughts about it with more or less likely conjectures—this is the principle of Acmeism"), and comments: "Thus Gumilev spoke. But there is no doubt that he subsequently abandoned this principle. For such verses as those just cited ["Stockholm"—ES] and some others that I have mentioned ["The Sixth Sense," "Memory," "The Word," "Soul and Body," "Primal Memory," "Nature"—ES] are precisely an attempt to know intuitively the unknowable. He who exclaimed 'Did I not love here and did I not die here!' can in no way be numbered among those who have renounced such attempts. It is another matter that Gumilev touches on the unknowable with Gumilevian

integrity and seriousness, through frugal and severe images and words."

46. See K. Mochul'skii, "Klassitsizm v sovremennoi russkoi poezii," *Sovremennye zapiski*, no. 11 (1922), 368–70.

47. N. Minsky's comment on the phases portrayed in "Memory" could be equally well applied to Gumilev's work as a whole: "And finally, the last phase—an inevitable return to mysticism, but no longer childishly naive, but consciously willed." See *Novaia russkaia kniga*, 1 (1922), p. 16.

48. Verkhovsky, p. 142.

Chapter Five

1. I have made an exception in the case of *The Path of Conquistadors*, since the three *poemy* in that book comprise such a central part of it—even physically, they are placed in the middle, between two sections of shorter lyric pieces—that it could hardly be discussed without including them.

2. Two excerpts from *Mik*, totaling eighty-four lines and headed "Two Passages from an Abyssinian Poem," were published in *The Quiver*.

3. *Apollon*, no. 5 (1914), p. 54; cf. SS, II, 335–36, where, however, the issue of *Apollon* is given erroneously as no. 1–2.

4. A. Gumileva, p. 123.

5. *Apollon*, loc. cit.

6. Strakhovsky, p. 31.

7. The extant fragments of the incomplete "Two Dreams" (II, 249–52) are not extensive enough to allow for any firm conclusions about the work, other than that it was to be a fantasy poem, intended for children, about the adventures of an eight-year-old Chinese girl. See SS, II, 342–43, for information on the dates of conception, writing, and posthumous publication of the fragments.

8. Translated in *The Abinger Garland*, pp. 16–21.

9. Cf. Isaiah 24:17: "Fear, and the pit, and the snare, are upon thee, O inhabitant of the earth." The origin of this line in Isaiah is indicated in Nadezhda Mandelstam, *Hope Against Hope*, p. 281.

10. *Hope Against Hope*, p. 198.

11. N. S. Gumilev, *Stikhotvoreniia. Posmertnyi sbornik* (Petrograd, 1923).

12. *Don Zhuan v Egipte* (Don Juan in Egypt) was first published in 1912, as part of *Foreign Skies*; it consists of 260 lines of iambic tetrameter, rhymed in quatrains. *Actaeon* was first published in 1913, in the Acmeist journal *Giperborey*. It consists of 240 lines of mostly

rhymed verse; the verse changes a number of times in the course of the play, alternating among several different meters. *Igra* (The Card Game) was first published in 1916, but is dated 1913 by the author; it contains only 75 lines of rhymed iambic tetrameters. The first two are subtitled "A One-Act Play in Verse"; *The Card Game* is subtitled "A Dramatic Scene."

13. Cf. Sam Driver, "Nikolaj Gumilev's Early Dramatic Works," *The Slavic and East European Journal*, XIII, 3 (1969), 326–47, for an analysis of the thematic unity of the plays, which, however, differs in certain important respects from the present analysis.

14. See S. Makovsky, "Nicolas Gumilev . . . ," p. 207; and SS III, 241–42.

15. SS III, 252. Professor Struve provides a careful and extremely valuable commentary to the play, including the history of the text and the historical background of the play (SS III, 245–92).

Selected Bibliography

PRIMARY SOURCES

Put' konkvistadorov (Petersburg, 1905).

Romanticheskie tsvety (Paris, 1908; 3rd ed. Petersburg: Prometei, 1918).·

Zhemchuga (Moscow: Skorpion, 1910; 2nd ed. Petersburg: Prometei, 1918; 3rd ed. Berlin: Mysl', 1921; 4th ed. Shanghai: Drakon, n. d.).

Chuzhoe nebo (Petersburg: Apollon, 1912; 2nd ed. Berlin: Petropolis 1936; 3rd ed. Shanghai: Drakon, n. d.).

Kolchan (Moscow-Petersburg: Giperborei, 1916; 2nd ed. Berlin: Petropolis, 1923).

Ditia Allakha (Petersburg: offprint from *Apollon*, 1918; 2nd ed. Berlin: Mysl', 1922).

Koster (Petersburg: Giperborei, 1918; 2nd ed. Berlin-Petersburg-Moscow: Z. I. Grzhebin, 1922; 3rd ed. Petersburg-Berlin: Z. I. Grzhebin, 1922).

Mik (Petersburg: Giperborei, 1918; 2nd ed. Petersburg: Mysl', 1921).

Farforovyi pavil'on (Petersburg: Giperborei, 1918; 2nd ed., augmented, Petersburg: Mysl', 1922).

Shater (Sevastopol: Tsekh poetov, 1921; 2nd ed. Petersburg-Revel: Bibliofil, 1922 {or 1921?}).

Ognennyi stolp (Petersburg: Petropolis, 1921; 2nd ed. Petersburg-Berlin: Petropolis, 1922).

Ten' ot pal'my. Rasskazy (Petersburg: Mysl', 1922).

Stikhotvoreniia. Posmertnyi sbornik (Petersburg: Mysl', 1922; 2nd ed., augmented, Petersburg: Mysl', 1923).

K sinei zvezde (Berlin: Petropolis, 1923).

Pis'ma o russkoi poezii (Petersburg: Mysl', 1923; 2nd ed. Shanghai, n. d.).

Posmertnye stikhi (Shanghai: Gippokrena, 1935).

Gondla (Berlin: Petropolis, 1936).

Izbrannye stikhi (Odessa, 1942).

The Abinger Garland. Nicolai Gumilev. Poems Translated from the Russian, trans. Yakov Hornstein (Dorking, England: *The Abinger Chronicle*, 1945).

185

Izbrannye stikhotvoreniia (Salzburg: Informatsionnyi biulleten', 1946).

Stikhotvoreniia v 4-kh tomakh, ed. V. Zavalishin (Regensburg, 1947–48).

Neizdannyi Gumilev, ed. G. P. Struve (New York: Chekhov Publishing House, 1952).

N. Gumilev. *Izbrannoe,* ed. N. Otsup (Paris: Librairie des cinq continents, 1959).

N. Gumilev. *Sobranie sochinenii,* ed. G. P. Struve and B. A. Filippov (Washington, D. C.: Victor Kamkin, 1962–68), 4 vols.

Selected Works of Nikolai S. Gumilev, trans. Burton Raffel and Alla Burago (no. 1 in the series *Russian Literature in Translation,* ed. Sidney Monas. Albany: SUNY Press, 1972).

Nikolai Gumilev on Russian Poetry, ed. and trans. David Lapeza (Ann Arbor, Mich.: Ardis, 1977).

SECONDARY SOURCES

Driver, Sam. "Acmeism." *The Slavic and East European Journal,* XII, 2 (1968), 141–56. The best summary of the history of the Acmeist school; clarifies, along roughly the same lines as the Weidlé article below, the points of continuity between Acmeism and Symbolism.

————. "Nikolaj Gumilev's Early Dramatic Works." *The Slavic and East European Journal,* XIII, 3 (1969), 326–47. An interesting, if perhaps a bit too schematic, analysis of the parallels between the early plays and the later ones. Particularly worthwhile for its indications of the subjective roots of the plays' central characters and their parallels with Gumilev's lyric poetry.

Ivanov, Georgii. "Blok i Gumilev," *Vozrozhdenie,* 6 (1949), 113–26. Probably the best treatment of the Blok-Gumilev juxtaposition, a recurrent theme in the émigré literature on Gumilev.

Makovskii, Sergei. "Nicolas Gumilev (1886–1921). Un témoignage sur l'homme et sur le poète." *Cahiers du monde russe et soviétique,* III, 2 (1962), 176–224. Combination of memoir and critical étude by the editor of *Apollon.* Interesting and provocative, although some of the critical interpretations and some points of Makovsky's understanding of Gumilev the man could be challenged. Also contains interesting material on the literary life of the period.

————. "Nikolai Gumilev," *Na Parnase "Serebrianogo veka."* (Munich: Verlag ZOPE, 1962), 195–222. Published earlier as "N. S. Gumilev" in *Grani,* 36 (Oct.–Dec. 1957). Major differences from the article above: does not contain nearly as much biographical and historical material; interpretations essentially the same.

MALINE, MARIE. *Nicolas Gumilev, poète et critique acméiste* (Brussels: Academie royale de Belgique, Classe des lettres et des sciences morales et politiques, tome LVII, fasc. 5, 1964). The only book-length study of Gumilev so far published. The chapter on his critical and theoretical views on poetry is of some value; the chapters on his life and poetry add little to what appeared in the short studies cited here.

MONAS, SIDNEY. "Gumilev: Akmê and Adam in Saint Petersburg," in *Selected Works of Nikolai S. Gumilev. Russian Literature in Translation 1,* Sidney Monas, ed. Albany: SUNY Press, 1972, pp. 3–26. A sensitive and perceptive essay; one of the best short articles on Gumilev, and *the* best in English.

ODOEVTSEVA, IRINA. *Na beregakh Nevy* (Washington, D.C.: Victor Kamkin, 1967). The many pages in this book devoted to Gumilev comprise the most extensive available memoir on him, and the richest in intimate details of everyday life, although of more significance are his reported comments on poetry, including his own work. Concerned mainly with the years 1919–21, but there is also information from earlier years.

OTSUP, NIKOLAI. "N. S. Gumilev." Preface to N. Gumilev, *Izbrannoe.* (Paris: Librairie des cinq continents, 1959). In two parts, the first biographical, the second analytical. The latter, which refutes many of the widespread misconceptions about Gumilev, takes the approach of dividing his poetry into a number of thematic cycles. Better than Otsup's 1953 *Opyty* article on Gumilev.

SECHKAREV, VSEVOLOD. "Gumilev-dramaturg." N. Gumilev, *Sobranie sochinenii,* ed. G. Struve and B. Filippov (Washington, D. C.: Victor Kamkin, 1966), III, iii–xxxvii. A brief section on the themes and patterns common to all the plays, followed by an analysis of each play individually. Together with the Driver article, basic to any further study of Gumilev's drama.

STRAKHOVSKY, LEONID. *Craftsmen of the Word. Three Poets of Modern Russia: Gumilev, Akhmatova, Mandelstam.* (1949; rpt. Westport, Conn.: Greenwood Press, 1969). The essay on Gumilev, which occupies about half of this small book, has the character of a biography-appreciation. Not entirely objective (Professor Strakhovsky was a friend and disciple of Gumilev), the essay is a noble tribute to the qualities of the man and poet. Heretofore the most extensive study of Gumilev in English. Very useful bibliography.

STRUVE, GLEB. "N. S. Gumilev: Zhizn' i lichnost'." *Sobranie sochinenii*, I, vii–lvi. The most accurate and complete biographical account. Quotes extensively from sources, including several reviews of Gumilev's earlier books.

————. "Tvorcheskii put' Gumileva." *Sobranie sochinenii*, II, v–xl. The best brief introduction to Gumilev; a systematic and objective survey of his whole literary career.

TUMPOVSKAIA, M. "Kolchan N. Gumileva," *Apollon*, 6–7 (1917), 58–69. Treats *Kolchan* as the turning point it was for Gumilev. Valuable for its criticism of the central weaknesses of his poetry as well as its insights into the strengths of Gumilev.

VERKHOVSKII, IURII. "Put' poeta. O poezii N. S. Gumileva." *Sovremennaia literatura*. Leningrad, 1925, pp. 93–143. An extremely thorough analysis of Gumilev's development as a poet. Emphasizes the gradual emergence of a genuine personal lyricism, and the resultant changes in the relationship between the lyric and epic strains; clarifies the effect of these processes on the poet's stylistics. The most perceptive piece of criticism yet written on Gumilev. Absolutely essential to a proper understanding of his poetry.

WEIDLÉ, WLADIMIR. "Peterburgskaia poetika." N. Gumilev, *Sobranie sochinenii*, IV, v–xxxvi. This excellent article puts Acmeism into a broader context than usual, showing its relationship to trends in the development of other, non-Acmeist poets; it also defines what the very different poets labeled Acmeists had in common.

ZHIRMUNSKII, VIKTOR. "Preodolevshie simvolizm," *Russkaia mysl'*, no. 12 (1916), 25–56. Reprinted with addenda in Zhirmunskii, *Voprosy teorii literatury* (The Hague: Mouton, 1962), 278–336. In contrast to the Driver and Weidlé articles, emphasizes the differences between Acmeism and Symbolism, and defines them very sharply, perhaps too schematically. The discussion of Gumilev's poetry is outdated and not especially perceptive, but retains some of its interest as an example of contemporary criticism which took the poet-warrior pose at face value.

Index

189